How to Become Extremely Successful in Business Management, Personal Management, and Family Budget Planning

2

How to Become Extremely Successful in Business Management, Personal Management, and Family Budget Planning

Dr. Udo F. Ufomadu, Ph.D.

U C & P

Published by:
U C & P
P.O. Box 746
Selma, AL 36702-0746

ISBN 0-9754197-0-6
Library of Congress Catalog Card Number: 2004093015

This book is dedicated to

my wife, Rita

my children, Evelyn, Joy, Ezekiel, and Godson

my brothers, James, Ike, and the late Godson

my sisters, Comfort, Peace, Esther, Edith, and Joy

my parents, the late Ezekiel & Evelyn Ufomadu,

my godchildren, Angel and Prince.

All of my uncles and aunts.

All of my brothers and sisters-in law.

All of my nieces, nephews, and cousins.

TABLE OF CONTENTS

PREFACE

This book actually celebrates the integration of motivational theories, success theories, and wisdom/understanding theories

The book is meant to help you upgrade yourself, upgrade family resources, and upgrade your business. The work is very encouraging and uplifting. It gives insight into problem-solving resources that actually exist, but have been overlooked or taken for granted. It did more than tell one to mow the lawn, for example, without giving the resources like lawn mower or grass cutter to do the job. It shows one how to develop enough personal power and eliminate self-defeating methods of growth and doing business. The fine analysis of the spiritual and the natural settings will compel you to recharge your self-confidence, and boost up your achievement level.

Furthermore, this book persuades you to take a hard look at what "success" really means to you. It encourages you to motivate your efforts toward reaching a realistic goal. By the time you get through with the entire book, you will definitely learn how to increase the value of yourself, your family, and/or your organization. You will develop new strategies for "success", build an unimaginable level of confidence, and elevate your problem-solving and decision-making skills. You will learn how to shape your management style to fit a particular problem that you want to solve, and not basing your approach on some sort of assumed or speculative circumstances. As a matter of fact, the best in you will come out and manifest itself by your new improvements, new ways of thinking, and new ways of doing things.

This work is for any age that can read. It tells you how to live a meaningful life. It also encourages you to seek meaningful associations and to improve your group or community by improving yourself first. It is absolutely impossible to achieve valid correctness from contentment with an incorrect self and uneducable status quo. People will change or improve if you are positive and your ideas are undeniably valuable.

More importantly, the book reminds you, through series of analogical paradigms, that success without wisdom from God in your life is like a water tank with an invisible leak. When you wake up in the morning, the water in your tank is gone and you cannot tell how or why.

You don't know because you just don't know. It is about time and it is never too late for us, my friends.

Read the book, take time to assimilate the quotations in the last chapter, and you'll be mightily enriched and utterly blessed.

Udo F. Ufomadu, Ph. D.

10

Chapter 1

MOTIVATING FOR EXCELLENCE

As the title of this chapter implies, this chapter is primed to motivate and empower a person to unlock the greatness in him or her and also ensure that those locks blocking his or her growth are thrown away for good. This work is specifically written to enhance the growth potential of myself, my family, my friends, anybody, and any business that is tired of silent contemplations. If you are tired of analysis without results, if you are tired of the devil-induced stagnancy, if you're fed up with the way things are going in your life or business, if you are utterly disappointed with the gross inappropriateness of a status quo, if you think or believe that you are not successful, this book is for you.

If you read and study this book in detail, including the quotations, it will prepare you on the necessary things you have to do relative to personal growth, family growth, acquiring a business, and growing a business. It will show you how to move from much talk to much action. It will show you where to get necessary support for financing your business, how to get a business plan, how to manage a business, how to market your business, and how to be able to comprehend the basic, but important, terms in a financial statement. It will also teach and show you the importance of family budget planning.

Family budget planning is an essential tool in making sure that a family enjoys their promise in its entirety. This area has been overlooked by a lot of families, but from a business standpoint, I think every family should practice it. In the latter part of this book, I will show you how to save and thereby, increase you/your family's net worth. You will be surprised how much wealth and self-esteem this book will instill in you and your family. It covers information for people with good credit standing and also helps people with fair or bad credit, such as where to get help if you've been turned down for a mortgage loan by traditional financial institutions, and how to manage your mortgage and other resources for optimum gain.

The benefits of this book will not manifest until you follow the basic teachings of the book and activate your stagnant plans. Motivate yourself adequately and induce yourself to action with wisdom from God.

God has promised to supply our needs according to His riches in glory by Christ Jesus. Still, we have to energize our supply base. As a matter of fact, the activation of your faith is the requirement for the easy flow of these supplies. It is disgusting for me to stack and pile my visions with no action. Of what value is my faith without action? It is repulsive when dreams are destroyed by fear of mortal disapproval. It is even an abomination when people whose needs have been supplied by God diminish for lack of courage. Nothing will occur until you make it occur. Even though Zacheus was invisible in the crowd, he took an unusual step. I strongly believe that immobile and non-modifiable plans cannot get you anywhere. Sometimes it takes an unusual but positive step to get what you want. I call Zacheus' move unusual because I don't believe that a chief among the publicans, who was rich, had originally planned to climb the Sycamore tree to see King Jesus. He evaluated his plan, found a problem and he reassessed his plan to include climbing the tree as a viable option of reaching his goal, which was seeing Jesus, regardless of what others thought. What he did was what I call "excluding the unwanted & including the needed" He deleted ego from his plan and added self-confidence. What was the outcome? Dining with God the Son.

Make your positive move today and disregard all mortals' negative disapprovals. All it takes in most cases is a vivid evaluation of your plan, your family plan, and a business plan if you're a business venture. Find out why you are not happy or successful, and then reassess your plan. When Zacheus discovered that the only reason he was not successful was because of his height, he looked for an answer, and meaningful results followed. Expert managers and good management consultants will agree with me on the fact that the only way to solving any problem is to first identify the problem.

Your business could be strategically located and have excellent credit ratings and connections, but suffer patriotism. Thorough evaluation of your problem could reveal that, for example, your employees lack the required business etiquette, particularly in the absence of management or any other person accountable for making profit. Some organizations or employers do not take time to educate their employees on the forms of conduct or behavior required to thrive reasonably in that particular business.

It is suitable at this point to state that the way a business treats their clients, and caters to their needs, determines their share of the community's economic harvests. The days of rigid approach are almost gone. Businesses and managers must adjust their management style to fit the needs of the people that make up their organization or community. Effective management, in my opinion, takes a considerable look at the situation at hand and not taking action based on a set assumption. You should spend considerable time on research, find out what your people need, work within your budget in providing such needs, and you'll be amazed at the return on your investment. For example, it will be a wrong business judgment to open up a hand crafted Italian shoe store that sells an average pair of shoes for $250.00 in a growing community that is dominated by minimum wage or slightly above minimum wage paying industries. You will motivate yourself wrongly by drawing inference from what goes on in a more established community without considering your community's present situation.

Furthermore, it is a wrong management assumption to start firing or laying off your trained employees in February of 2004 because business was very slow in March 2003. There are many more examples. You can contact my consulting firm if you need help.

I have included in this book some *terrific* motivational quotes, which businesses and individuals should draw strength from. They are none of those quotes that an individual will find difficult to comprehend. These quotes are for children as well as adults. All you have to do is back it up with wisdom from the word of God. These quotes will implant in you the right values necessary for dealing with yourself, your family, an organization you belong to, your employees, your supervisors, fellow associates, and the job itself.

This book also did its best by encouraging entities to back themselves up with basic ammunition necessary for thriving in today's world. Since technology has swept almost all aspects of job performance, basic education like computer or accounting knowledge is now a necessity. It is also good for businesses to educate employees on the general forms of having a successful enterprise. Of emphasis, and worthy of restating, is the fact that it is best when you harmoniously combine your education with wisdom and understanding. The Bible actually tells us that the fear of God is the beginning of wisdom. More so, that obedience to the word of God is a guaranteed success. Think about that. If you are wise, you are prone to be successful. The mastery of a relationship with the Owner of everything that I want should come first, before the mastery of everything that He owns. Piece of cake.

God's connection will link you to the right people to do business with. Even if you find yourself in the wrong hands, God will drench you with wisdom to pull through. If you intentionally use God's word disapprovingly in your dealings to cheat people, you are certainly sowing bad seeds. Consequently, you should expect bad harvests. Businesses and individuals will be overly successful if they combine the business principles learned in seminars and colleges with God's principles (wisdom and understanding).

There are lots of misconceptions about success. The Webster's dictionary defined success as the gaining of wealth, the gaining of fame, prosperity, achievement, and gaining the price aimed at. It also defined motivation as an input that induces or drives a person to achieve and also as an incentive. Prior to writing this book, I researched and did a well-tailored survey to determine what success means to others and also ascertain factors that motivate students, professionals, children, teenagers, and adults in the 21st century.

Before looking at what these people think about motivation and success, it will be pertinent at this early stage for me to define both subjects in my own terms. *Motivation,* to me, is any factor that ensures that Dr. Udo Ufomadu will put his utmost abilities to use for optimum achievement. You can delete Dr. Udo Ufomadu's name and insert yours. *Success*, to me, is when my God is happy, my family is happy, and I am happy.

There are numerous definitions for success and I believe each person should define success for himself or herself. It should never be based on what others think, what the society thinks, or some sets of assumptions.

It is important at this point to look at how others have responded. I will only disclose the names of responders that gave me the permission to do so. The survey ranges from that of an elementary student to that of a Chief Executive Officer (CEO) of a business firm. They were all asked the same questions. The questions were "How do you define success?" and "How do you motivate yourself or others to achieve?"

The first responder is Daniel Anyanwu, who is the Chief Executive Officer of these three business entities, Dixie Loan & Mortgage Inc., Checks-2-Cash, Wares Ferry Accounting Inc., told me that success for him is when his organizations can appropriately satisfy their clients without taking advantage of them financially. He said that any transaction that adequately satisfies his organization and his clients is a success to him. He asserted that the only true definition for success is hard work.

He motivates his employees by instilling feeling of importance in them.

The second responder is Ms. Liz Rutledge, a Regions Bank manager in Selma, Alabama. She said, " I feel successful every time that I achieve the goals that I set for myself. My spirituality is success to me. Having my only son is success to me." "We motivate our employees with free lunch, monetary rewards, and other incentives."

Third person is Barbara Sanders, The director of critical care at Vaughan Medical Center. "I feel successful when someone comes into the hospital very sick and leaves feeling 100 percent better" Positive outcomes motivate me.

Fourth person:

"Success means leaving this job for another job." "Money motivates me."

Fifth responder:

"Success means to hit lottery." "Money motivates me."

Sixth responder:

"Success means a man building his life according to the word of God." "My family motivates me."

Seventh responder:

"You are successful any time you find yourself working for yourself." " Increase in finance will motivate me."

Eighth responder:

"I feel successful in knowing that I'm saved." "God's word motivates me."

Ninth responder is Mr. Rufus Watkins, an industrial supervisor:

"Money, health, and sex are success." "I'm motivated when people appreciate me."

Tenth responder, Dr. Daniel Kalu, a businessman:

"Success is my educational achievements, being married at 25 which has not been interrupted for 32 years, becoming a millionaire at 30, and becoming born again when I was a child." "My family motivates me."

Eleventh responder:

"Success is a home paid for, couple of vehicles, and acres of land paid for." "Money motivates me."

Twelfth responder:

"Knowing that all my needs are met makes me successful." "Love motivates me."

Thirteenth responder:

"Reaching my goals and becoming what I want to be. To prove to naysayers as well as encouragers that I can do it, is an incentive for me." "Money and family motivate me."

Fourteenth responder:

"To accomplish all of my life goals, be a light to others, knowing the Lord and putting Him first, and being saved." "My companion motivates me."

Fifteenth responder:

"Success means being able to fulfill your dreams." "My parents' success motivates me."

Sixteenth responder:

"Doing something right is success." "My mother motivates me."

Seventeenth responder is Mr. Ricky Brown, an industrial manager and a preacher:

"Being able to bless people financially and spiritually without pressure is success." "Expecting God to bless me financially and spiritually motivates me."

Eighteenth responder, Mr. Oge Onuoha, a pharmacist/pharmacy technician:

"Success is when you get to your stated goals." "Results of the goals motivate me."

Nineteenth responder is Mr. J. Brooks, a preacher:

"Not material things." "Being in a good relationship with God motivates me."

Twentieth responder is Mrs. Glenda Williams, a businesswoman of God:

"Success is fulfilling your dreams and having a little bit more to give others and to use." "Making a difference in somebody's life motivates me."

Twenty-first responder is Mr. L. Page, an industrial foreman and a church deacon:

"Knowing that I'm saved is success for me." "My family motivates me"

The twenty-second person is Mr. Wayne Stone, a successful State/USDA Inspector In Charge of R. L. Zeigler Incorporated once told me, while we were coming home from a meeting, that his extreme success stories include, but not limited to, having a good family, being able to teach the word of God in his church, becoming a church deacon, and his unremitting spiritual growth. The love of God and love for his family motivates him to achieve the natural and the spiritual.

The twenty-third responder is Mr. Ralph Hathcock, a successful Consumer Food Safety Protection Specialist and a prolific investor:

"My wife of 38 years is success to me. I have been able to raise my children safely in today's dangerous world. My children have not gotten themselves in any kind of trouble that bothered me. This is extreme success for me." "My family motivates me to keep working hard"

The twenty-fourth responder is Chief Consultant, Emmanuel Epeagba, of Emmanuel & E Accounting, Inc. He said, "Success is reaching my set goals." "Money motivates me."

In an exclusive interview by the author with Emmanuel C. Oranika, Ph.D., the Metropolitan and Statewide Transportation Planning

Engineer/Assistant Bureau Chief of Alabama
Department of Transportation, Dr. Oranika
explicitly explained how he became extremely
successful. He said that he became exceptionally
successful when he gave his life to Jesus. He holds
series of college degrees, including a doctorate in
Engineering. He has held important titles as a leader
or president of organizations. He travels nationally
and internationally. Moreover, he has a beautiful
family, which I can attest to. From all indication, he
is successful. But he feels extremely successful each
time he remembers that he is Heaven-bound. He
turned his back on the devil and his plans and held
Christ tight. By the author's theory, he excluded the
unwanted and included the needed in an effort to
become extremely successful. He continued by
saying that he has immensely gained a lot by giving
himself to Christ. Dr. Oranika said that God in
return revealed himself to him by letting him know
that Doc. can do anything that he set his mind to do.
Dr. Oranika undoubtedly believes that he is one of
those children that have been ordered to go and
increase, multiply, and dominate the world.

In a special interview with Mel Gibson by
Peggy Noonan, in the Reader's Digest, Gibson
clearly indicated that his search for spiritual growth
motivated him to make the movie called *Passion.*
The idea for the movie incubated in him for 12
years according to Gibson. He said that even though
he has everything that money can afford, even
though he makes good movies, and even though he
has a good family, something was still missing in
his success package. He could not become
extremely successful until he evaluated and

reassessed his plan accordingly. He said, " I might look like I'm living the high life, making movies and jetting around the world. But true happiness resides within. I was spiritually bankrupt, and when that happens, it's like a spiritual cancer afflicts you. It starts to eat its way through, and if you don't do something, it's going to take you. So I simply had to draw a line in the sand."

     I, the author, had the blessing of being the son of the owner of now defunct E. E. Ufomadu & Sons' Contractors. He was a God fearing man and a pioneer member of the Assemblies of God in Nigeria. A lot of younger businessmen in his days looked up to him for an advice and as a role model. Many that he worked with succeeded spiritually and materially. When he left to be with the Lord, materially, I inherited two brick houses, a plantation and acres of land. Spiritually I inherited a path with immeasurable value. Mr. E. E. Ufomadu once explained how he included the needed and excluded the unwanted in an effort to become extremely successful. His business moved from shipping food products between regions to becoming a building contractor. While the former business gave him more wealth, the latter gave him enough wealth, an opportunity to spend more time with his family, an opportunity to serve the Lord with his money and through offices held in the Christian community, and an opportunity to sow in the lives of newly wedded couples in wedding ceremonies that he was called to be the Chairman of the occasion in almost every weekend. Mr. E.E. Ufomadu enjoyed it because he loved young couples and would do whatever he could to support them through word of wisdom and financially. Worthy of note is the fact that he was more successful with the accomplishment that came with the latter business, even with a decreased finance.

The founder of Tabernacle of Praise, my pastor, was a college dean when I met him 1997. As a matter of fact, he rose to the rank of an Acting President of the college. At that point, most people thought that he was extremely successful as a pastor of a great church and a college dean/acting college President. But to their uttermost surprise, he retired at 45 years from the college to face his pastorship full-time. Mr. Efell Williams excluded the unwanted and included the needed to become extremely successful. He evaluated his plan and knew exactly what ultimate happiness and success meant to him at that point in life. He forfeited the worldly status and all the money that he was making at the college in exchange for extreme success. He now has the opportunity to pastor the way God wants him to, which is more fulfilling to him. This great success reflects on everything around him.

Another excellent example is that of the founder of Ministering Monologues Inc. She and her family are our friends, so I know her story well. She has a Bachelor's Degree in Speech Communications and Theater, she was a featured dancer on the T.V. show *Soul Train*, had an acting role in *The Heat of the Night* and *Matlock,* was featured in several commercials, has held the crown for a statewide pageantry, has worked as manager for a distribution company, and was a school teacher when she quit her teaching job to become what I call "extremely successful". Despite all of these human acclamations and approbations, these were not considered complete success to Mrs. Denise Dukes. She reassessed her plan to exclude the unwanted and include the needed. The resultant effect is happiness and sense of accomplishment. This former actress, dancer, manager, and teacher now uses her ministry to entertain and at the same time change lives. The people that know her personally can attest to the fact that there is something different in her life. Her life is more meaningful and adequate.

The last three examples are not encouraging you to quit your present career in order to find extreme success. You can find success in your present career by paying attention to the 99 percent positive in your job and overlooking the one percent negative. Success can come by the enrichment of your hobby, your part-time endeavors, or your spirituality. Just include the needed. It could mean the inclusion of quality prayer and superior love in your lifestyle.

In my own case, I, the author, have always known that something was missing in my extreme success package. I love my family, I love my job, I love my friends, I'm comfortable with my spiritual growth, but still I can feel a deficiency of one percent missing in my package for excessive success. I shared this with God, family and few friends. I have always enjoyed using a brain storming approach in chasing a goal. I do not restrict myself. Once I have discussed it with God, I will step out in faith and make several positive attempts until I find His perfect will for me. For example, after receiving my Bachelor of Science in

Business Administration and a Master of Science in Administration and Supervision, I did not restrict my job search to Business or Educational Management. No wonder I have made a successful career inspecting and regulating meat food products for the government and the consumers. We should not restrict ourselves if we are certain that we can do all things through Christ who empowers us. Despite all these worldly acquisitions, with included obtaining a Doctorate in Business Administration, I still knew within me that one percent deficiency has to be taken care of. It was eating me up. I know that I cannot pay God back for his goodness in my life but I desperately wanted a genuine avenue that God will use me in making a difference in people's life. Moreover, I wanted an endeavor that will bring me utter satisfaction and joy. On my own, I made so many constructive efforts to fill my one percent gap. Nothing really changed until I reassessed my plan to include giving God complete control and He took my consulting/writing work to the next level. As a matter of fact, inspirational writing then, was the least area that I had expected to fill my one percent gap. The point here is that I tried a lot of things by my own power without evaluating my plan. No wonder much did not come out of it. As soon as I rearticulated my plan and excluded the unwanted and included the needed, things began to flow smoothly. I actually excluded the fear of mortal disapproval and included the total control of God and I became very happy. God uses my writings to inspire. Never have I ever attained this degree of success that I am convinced that it incontrovertibly makes my God happy, makes my family happy, makes my friends happy, and makes me happy. Like I have always said, I feel very successful whenever I can genuinely make my God, my family, my friends, and myself proud. I know that this is just the preamble of God's plan for my life. I strongly believe that this is an introduction of a whole new book on my journey. Even though I may not know exactly what path that God leads me next, all that I feel is abundance of goodness. Certainly, all that I see is enough, and excess, of God's favor.

My books have not given me millions of dollars yet, but they have given me immense joy. I have hugely enjoyed writing down my personal and other people's experiences so that the younger and the older generations will learn and improve their lives and organizations.

My wife can testify to the joy I had when a lady that I have never met before stopped us at Winn-Dixie and told me how my book has blessed her. As a matter of fact, she told my wife and me that she would buy any other book that I will write.

My son's principal, Ms. Burton, told me what my book meant to her. I thanked God.

I was very grateful to God when an associate, Theresa, called from Birmingham Alabama to tell me how valuable the book is to her and her friends.

I was very appreciative to God one Thursday night when a nurse case manager said, "Don't stop inspiring me." There are many such instances but they are not the point here. The point here is that a plan was evaluated and action was taken based on the outcome of the evaluation. The result is complete joy for my family, my friends, and me. I thank God that He chose even me to prove His supremacy.

So based on these examples, I can easily conclude that different things motivate or enthuse different people. Furthermore, people see success differently.

Relying on my analysis, I will strongly suggest that each reader should honestly define success for himself or herself in order to be satisfied with his or her achievement. You really have to be candid with yourself. Each of us has certain degrees of success in us. You cannot let the one percent insufficiency outshine the 99 percent sufficiency. If you discover that something is missing in your package for extreme success, tell God about it and make a move right now, babe. You can draw positive inference from series of examples given in this book. God already told us His thoughts towards us. So the question is what are your thoughts towards closing the gap? If you don't make that move or redefine success today, you may spend all your life chasing success when happiness is close by staring at you. If after much examination of your self, you still couldn't find success, the next paragraphs may be of immense help.

Based on my study and experience, I can authoritatively affirm that the first step to success is having a good foundation. The second step is to have a plan and set realistic goals. If you are a business venture, have a well-documented business plan that will show where you are today and where you want to be tomorrow. Even if you are not a business entity, you want to know where you are going.

My formula, P+P+W= EX, is explained as Pray + Plan +Wait =Enough and Excess. If your plan is rooted around prayer and the word of God, which is a good foundation, if your plan is well-organized, and if you wait and listen carefully for God's perfect will and make adjustments accordingly, the resultant effects are nothing but satisfaction and excess (extreme success).

We all know that God's plan is best for our lives; still we have the responsibility of making this plan work. It is God's plan for us to stay healthy, but we must eat healthy and exercise. It is God's plan for food to digest in our stomach, but remember, the food has to be properly cooked and sometimes checked or swallowed by us, not God, before it gets to our stomach. We absolutely have a part to play in making sure that our life reaches its potential.

The same principle applies to all aspects of our relationship and survival. One more time, faith without action is questionable. Your first move to success is the first move you make.

Reset your goal, if necessary. By this, I mean that people or businesses should dream big, yet have realistic objectives. For example, it will be meaningless for an immigrant U.S. citizen to aspire to be a president of the United States when you already know that the present Constitution, as of the writing of this book, excludes immigrant citizens. Furthermore, it will be repulsive to aspire to be a physician, an engineer, an accountant, a computer programmer, a chiropractor, a Ph.D. or other doctoral professional, a pharmacist, a lawyer, a veterinarian, a food safety specialist, a nurse, a judge, a schoolteacher or a principal, etc., when you have excluded attending college in your plans. Similarly, it will be revolting for an individual to aspire to be extremely successful in business without finance or any kind of business plan. Also, it will be horrendous to exclude regular practices from your plan if you intend to be a professional or real good at what you do.

Besides the above-mentioned instances, there are many other aspirations that an individual can include in his or her plans and become extremely successful if he or she does not ignore the obligatory basics vital to excelling in such endeavors.

A man can start by aspiring to be the best father or husband, which is the fundamental of all successes. This is a leadership role in the highest. Also, a woman can start by aspiring to be the best wife or mother that has ever lived. This is a management role with immense dignity. If you are able to love, provide, and co-manage your family to happiness, you should consider yourself a success. See yourself as the President or Manager of your family. Remember, a good manager is that successful coach who knows how to get players to play together for one purpose. Good management skill is a necessity in the planning and in the attaining stages.

For example, if you are a startup business, your lenders may want to know the type of management team that you are putting together to ensure that their money will be recovered. Even if you are not seeking financial help, you still want good employees in order to have an edge over your competition. Good employees are the key to your business success.

How to Attract and Retain Good Team Members/Employees

Hiring and retaining good employees are a necessary and difficult function of a human resources planner. While the personnel manager or the human resources manager of an established firm may have an idea of what to do, the small business man or woman may not know what to do. These are some of my clues, based on what an average good worker thinks. These facts were acquired as a participant observer, as a soccer captain who recommended the hiring and retaining of good players for employment, as a management consultant, and some were gained through research/survey methods. My clues will give a business or a manager some insight on things that you have to do to attract and keep the best.

• I believe that most good employees want their employment to be unwavering.

• I know that an achiever will prefer a position that will allow him or her to make substantial use of his/her gained experiences.

• All good employees that I researched on or that I have known prefer jobs with a future.

• I strongly believe that every employee wants to be treated with some level of respect.

• It is my conclusion that good people prefer an employer who listens to what they have to say. A boss that cares.

• I am very sure that good employees prefer managers who know how to deal with people fairly, without favoritism. Managers who do not bring their biases to the work place. Managers who will reward an input without being told to.

• Similar to the point before this, is the fact that good employees actually reach out to jobs that give them equal opportunity. You will be surprised, if you find out how much these prospective employees research on employer's reputation.

• I am sure that workers, regardless of their background, prefer jobs that provide benefits. Even if you are a small business, you can still provide a type of group insurance. You can have a family support account, to help families with emergency and unexpected needs. During the time that I was writing this book, I interviewed a Chief Executive Officer (CEO), who told me that on a regular basis he buys free lunch for his employees. This may show that he cares, even though that he thinks some of his employees do not appreciate it. The employees that do not appreciate the lunch may want the gesture in the form of cash. This point is one of the reasons that I have emphasized on the fact that an employer or manager should know the most suitable option for your situation or employees before trying to motivate them.

• Like I mentioned earlier, a prospective employee's research on an organization can reveal to them if they have a chance to advance in an organization or not. People will be motivated to work and contribute largely to an organization if they are sure that they will receive fair treatment for their sacrifices and contributions to the organization. Some people have told me that they will never work for certain organizations, despite the fact that these organizations offer better pay.

• I am certain that most employees like to be recognized for things that they have done. Present and even past achievements. These same employees do not like a boss who will not forget their past mistakes. A boss who will withhold a present reward in exchange for a past, maybe corrected, mistake.

• I believe that all good employees, regardless of their background, seek out those jobs that will elevate their present conditions. They want jobs that will necessarily improve his or her family's present standard of living.

• Finally, I am of the strong estimation that good workers prefer a leader who will listen and give them an opportunity to participate, in some kind of way, in decision-making that affects them and their job.

Management By Objective (MBO)

Managers who involve their employees in the decision-making process are using a type management approach called Management By Objective (MBO). Because I like this management style, I will spend a little time on it. With MBO, an employee participates in goal setting. It is amazing to know how much this approach can motivate employees.

The good part about MBO is that the workers know what the management expects from them when the projected period starts. The fact that the employees are not taken by surprise is fulfilling. Some employees simply enjoy the fact that they are given the chance to talk with their supervisor(s) or manager(s) about issues concerning them. This serves as a great motivator.

During one of my trips to Africa, a client complained to me about the high degree of loss his business was experiencing. I looked at his financial statement and discovered that most of his records looked great. I opted to observe his employees and possibly talk to some. I sure did. My observation came out to be what I expected. These employees were actually afraid of him. Nobody, in his absence knew what was expected to be done in the next 15 minutes. Nobody in his absence had been trained enough to answer the basic question concerning their jobs. Most contracts were verbal and employment was terminated easily. The employees pretended to be busy when they were really not. Based on these few minutes of observations, I figured out exactly why he was at loss.

During our next meeting, I did not go in details on my observation in fear of the fact that his retribution on his employees may backfire and result in a complete closure of the business.

But what I did share with him was the advantages of MBO. First, he was very adamant about the whole issue. He said that I should use an African approach for African employees. "This is not America," he said. I convinced him to just try. Eventually he did and the result was happiness and satisfaction for himself and his workers. His business actually became profitable.

In about six months he contacted and detailed me on his new expansion based on the MBO approach. His employees became satisfied with their job and consequently produced beyond expectation.

MBO helps the worker to know that his/her performance affects the overall achievement of the organization, thereby instilling a feeling of importance in the individual. By giving them a chance to be involved in goals affecting them, they know exactly what the organizational leaders expect from them. These workers know exactly what goals that they are preparing to reach. Moreover, they have the understanding of how their performance will be evaluated. This style motivates employees; this management style takes away the suspicion of unfair treatment always aimed at the management because each employee now knows what he or she is sowing as a seed as much as s/he knows what s/he will reap. More importantly, it leaves the line of communication open. It undoubtedly improves employer-employee communication, which is very essential to the achievement of any organizational goals and objectives.

Barbara Sanders, the director of Critical Unit in Vaughan Medical Center, the manager of more than 38 nurses, with other demands that come with managing a department, acknowledges that she is very happy, as at the writing of this book, with the present hospital administration. As she puts it, "The administration listens to us. I know we have their support. We are considered to be part of the team." You cannot beat this. This is an outstanding example of the effect of a management team that listens and involves their employees in the decision making process.

In similar instance that buttresses the importance of involving and appreciating your employees, Mrs. Vera Anyanwu the Managing Director of United Food Outlet Incorporated, confirmed to me that the enormous cooperation and efforts that she has been enjoying from her employees stem from the fact that she constantly reminds her employees through action and word of mouth that everybody is important to the organization. Moreover, that everybody's contribution or suggestion is needed. This leadership style enhances employee self-esteem and thereby promotes productivity.

I have my simple quote to crown this fact. "Happy employees produce happy results."

Contingency Approach to Management

Another favorite management style of mine is the contingency management style. Just like other management principles, there may not be a written rule to being a perfect organizational or family manager. Management decision is based on the available resources and situation at hand. This is sometimes called the situational approach to management. A man named Fred Fiedler developed the contingency theory of leadership. The theory stipulates that there is no best way to lead. A particular situation will decide the approach or alternative to use. A contingency approach requires the planner to make excellent choices, given the best estimate of the situation at hand. Read the following chapter on planning, for guides on how to elevate your family's net worth. You have to apply certain management principles based on your family's situation. On the other hand, you have to master your relationship with your family, spend quality time with each other, pray and have devotions together, and find out the cost of each member's expected needs. The next chapter advises and shows how family budget planning will lead to extreme financial success.

But we are not finished yet with motivation. A person can be motivated to be the best father, mother, grandfather, grandmother, sister, brother, uncle, aunt, cousin, nephew, and niece in your family circle. "Best" here can only be defined by you. It may me wrong to define it in terms of monetary value. "Best" for me are those quality packages that enhance the spiritual and normal well being of your organization or family circle. This is an achievable goal that is worth setting. It is a prize that deserves to be aimed at. A kind of goal that will make any right-minded individual happy. You become a joy to your family unit. As a result, success is achieved for reaching that honor aimed at, and not for becoming wealthy or rolling in it. Your newfound success/happiness will reflect on almost everything that you do.

Furthermore, you can aspire to be the best member of your group, regardless of your position in that team. Team or group here refers to your job, your church, your society, your sports group, investment group, and other organizations that you may be part of. You do not have to be an official/management team of your organization or group to be of importance. You do not have to be a minister in your church in order to be of value and consequently become successful. Your presence can bring peace to your group because you are already rooted in harmony. Your presence can bring hope because you are a person of faith. Your presence can bring laughter and smile on faces that would have been otherwise languishing in frustration. Your presence can bring love to your group by way of reconciling differences in group settings. Just try, aspire, and bring something to the table.

Another way of being successful in a group setting is based on your ability to master the individuals in your group. This is of extreme importance. You definitely do not want to remain in a group that does not want you to succeed, unless you do not have a choice. I advocate unity among family regardless of most situations. The goodness in you can turn things around in a bad group. Some people in a group are actually worse than Judas Iscariot. By this I mean they can betray you without even asking for a penny. Betrayal actually affects trust and consequently retards growth. Growth as we know, does not thrive well in a divided team.

It is worthy to know that great team players or successful players, cover the mistake of a fellow player during a game, but talk it over after the game, or forgive and forget about it.

One of my favorite motivational quotes is the one Jesus, God the Son, quoted in Mathew 7:7, "Knock and it shall be opened to you." On the other hand, if you do not knock, the door will not opened. If you do not act, nothing will react. What a simple but powerful illustration for attaining spiritual and normal success.

As a matter of fact, I have always been fascinated by motivation and planning. As a result, most of my research works in Bachelor of Science, Masters, and Doctorate programs centered on motivation and planning.

Through my researches now and then, I came to the conclusion that different things motivate different people.

During my undergraduate program, my management professor was disappointed when I told him that money is the ultimate motivator. On the other hand, I was extremely disappointed at him when he suggested that a personal parking space could serve as a motivator. I have used this illustration to cement the fact that it is not responsible to look down on people based on what motivates them and what success really means. Let God make that distinction. If you believe they need help, aid them and God will bless you. For me, at that college student level, a restaurant employee, who made $3.50 an hour, without benefits, to pay for school fees, buy books, live in an apartment, and pay the utilities that come with it, money was the only thing that could motivate me. But as for my instructor, a high-ranking official in the Gunter Air Force Base in Alabama, and a part-time college instructor, a personal parking space is a motivator. Regardless of how I try to justify my response, money is not the ultimate motivator. Personal parking space, that I enjoy now, is a motivator. Money, family, spirituality, and many more factors of motivation worthy to be looked at in the following chapters are all great incentives.

My point here is that it is best for you to wear shoes that fit your feet perfectly or they will affect your walk. By this, I mean an individual should find out exactly what's most convenient for him/herself, his/her family, and his/her organization. You must find out what motivates you at each level, and find out what God's perfect will for your life is. A fine analysis of all these, will to a large extent determine how you define success. Money is a motivating factor and may be a necessary ingredient. I am of the estimation that money alone cannot make some one successful. If you become too wealthy and lack God and management skills to manage it to victory, it can ruin your life by becoming a god for you. If your family needs food and shelter, the only feasible motivator is any positive job that pays money. Your leadership capability will be classified as a failure if you intentionally refuse to make a move and get a job. Success for you and your family at that point is food and shelter. If these fundamentals are successfully carried out, God will then promote you to the next level. Remember, promotion that stays comes from God. "For promotion cometh neither from the east, nor from the west, nor from the south. But God is the judge: he putteth down one, and setteth up another," Psalms 75:6-7.

Chapter 2

THEORIES OF
MOTIVATION & SUCCESS

This chapter explores four conclusions by four researchers. Three of these theories are from world-renowned theorists, and a conclusion from the author, Dr. Ufomadu. These four concepts are not chosen for comparison sake, rather they are carefully chosen for learning and upgrading purposes.

Some highly celebrated researchers, like Maslow, Herzberg, and McClelland, have made outstanding contributions in the field of motivation that their works are, constantly, made reference to by students, teachers, practitioners, and consultants.

Maslow's Theory

Maslow's theory stipulates that people tend to be motivated when you satisfy their basic needs. His hierarchy arranges motivational needs in order of priority. Maslow actually came up with what is called Maslow's Need Theories of Motivation, which are physiological needs, security and belonging needs, and self-actualization needs.

The physiological needs include things like food, water, road and shelter.

The security needs refers to protection and avoidance of harm.

What A.H. Maslow actually preached was that an individual whose family lacks food, water, and shelter to survive would not be interested in prestige, status, or community power. My survey agreed with his argument to a large extent, but there are some people that I know that have completely different opinions.

What Maslow postulated in his theory of human motivation is true, but if he were alive today, he would have discovered that a lot of individuals or businesses have opted to fly instead of climbing. I know a nation that wants to be a super power when the citizens of that country cannot afford running water and electricity. We know some countries that spend millions on jets/ ammunitions when the citizens of such countries lack sufficient food and roads. This is either a poor management style in practice, or acts of being negatively motivated as Maslow predetermined. Another reason for such leadership style, in my judgment, may be the fact that the leaders of such countries may have satisfied their own basic needs like water, light, food and shelter and do not care where the masses stand on the hierarchy of needs theory. If this is the case, leadership has to be redefined for these elected officials. Any time that an individual or group of individuals are entrusted with the management of a community or a country's resources, such group is responsible for the equitable distribution of such resources. A nation is like any other entity. A country or its branches should be managed based on the condition of such nation and its available resources, and not based on some ridiculous and unreasonable postulation.

Herzberg's Theory

Another renowned theorist known as Frederick Herzberg came up with the conclusion that people tend to be motivated, particularly, in an organization if you positively incorporate achievement, recognition, responsibility, and advancement in their duty. My survey had a lot of people agreeing with this concept. But some Christians I interviewed saw it differently. These Christians expect two-dimensional routes to their achievement and advancement. They are more interested in the factors that will help them to advance and achieve in spiritual and natural realms. Some are less interested in the natural.

McClelland's Theory

A well-known Harvard psychologist, David C. McClelland, gathered a group of researchers in 1940 in an attempt to discover things that actually motivate people to achieve or reach their potential. McClelland centered his work on achievement-oriented individuals. By the way, achievement oriented individuals are more likely to translate their thoughts into action. He believed that achievement oriented people do not take high risks. They usually take well-calculated risks according to McClelland. Such people believe that their goals are reachable and success is almost certain. They disagree with the fact that success is tied to short-term endeavors. Moreover, they are always interested in ascertaining how good they are doing. They really will like to know how things are coming up with their ventures.

Of significant relevance to McClelland's conclusion is the fact that parental influence helps to mold these achievement-oriented individuals. These individuals tend to come from parents who set very high standards for achievement. These parents support their goals through action and encouragement without being overly authoritative. These parents maintain visible uniformity in the way they discipline their children. Discipline is focused and based on what a child did.

Another area of McClelland's conclusion that is of immense importance to me is the notion that people's decision not to do better can be a result of an association, a group, or a culture that the individual is part of. This particular emphasis gets a support from Proverbs 13:20,"He that walketh with wise men shall be wise: but a companion of fools shall be destroyed." I definitely, agree with McClelland and the Bible. There is no doubt to the fact that what goes into a child's head today, helps to mold him or her for tomorrow. Who we closely associate ourselves with, affects our achievement level.

My advice to businesses, as a consultant, is that you need to find out what your workers needs are at any particular time. You can refer to my suggestions on how to get and retain good team members/employees. If you give them what they need, they most likely will remain with you loyally. Find out what you can give that will give you an edge over your competitors. Based on my survey, I can easily conclude that the key factor for everybody is "need". Everyone that I talked to has a need to satisfy. Even some very spiritual persons, who mightily impressed me with high level of satisfaction, still have needs that have to be serviced. Besides spiritual needs, all of them want their respective families to be happy. These are some of the things employers or organizational heads take for granted, and in most cases, suffer the consequences. As far as business growth is concerned, I suggest that a business owner should take time to master their businesses, evaluate their business plan constantly, and make adjustments whenever necessary. If you don't have a business plan, I suggest that you get a well-written plan soon. Success takes God, planning, hard work, and some time. Treat your clients with respect, regardless of their background. If you have clients from a different nationality, try to know a little bit of their culture. Just use the word of God positively as it applies to your business. With prayer and God on your side, I believe success is guaranteed.

For individuals, I advise that you define success, as it will be meaningful to you at any particular stage. Don't see success as being a millionaire, a CEO or a company's president. Success goes beyond title and cash. Your family may be in need of a CEO and a family President. Be good at any choice you make. Try your best to be upright in your dealings with people. The Bible tells us that anybody that diligently seeks good procureth favor. See yourself as a success at the family level. Wanting to fly instead of climbing is motivating yourself negatively. Consequently, your failure will affect your self-esteem. You will be ultimately pulling yourself down which will impact your self-esteem adversely in a very negative manner. If you continue to pull yourself down, the devil will help you in the attempt to destroy yourself. The devil will certainly blow your weaknesses and failures out of proportion. Please read and assimilate my quotations in the last chapter. They will help to serve as additional compasses that guide your life or businesses' journey. The quotes are not arranged or divided between individuals and businesses for this reason. Individuals make up businesses. Moreover, businesses cannot function in the absence of human resources. Every quote is beneficial to human or business existence. These are quotes for every level of humanity. From children to parents, elementary to college students, intending husbands to intending wives, and husband to wives.

Once again, I encourage, my family, myself, and others to stay away from choices that will negatively impact self-esteem, thereby jeopardizing growth possibilities. Remember, if you motivate yourself adequately you will have meaningful success.

The energy expended on destroying yourself could be spent in enjoying success, praising and worshipping God, sipping on alcohol-free Spumante, iced tea, or a cool glass of water.

Author's Research Observation

A thorough analysis of my research led me to conclude that spiritual people, like faithful Christians, consider themselves to be already successful and are easily motivated to achieve. Without much thought, the entire spiritual minded responders knew exactly what their goals and objectives are. These Christians seem to have success that could not be taken away from them by another individual. Most that I interviewed, categorically, identified two successes. These two successes are the spiritual and the natural. I call the spiritual " major'', and the natural I call "minor''. I came up with this concept based on the responses that I received from those surveyed. A church deacon said this: " being saved is the only success that I know. My family motivates me to seek the natural.'' A preacher told me that he feels successful any time that he finds himself giving to others spiritually and naturally.

Many of these Christians believe that once the "major" is taken care of, the "minor" will easily unwrap itself. They believe that the covenant and promises that God has for His children motivate them to live righteous. The attachment to the Creator, by itself, is seen as a success by these Christians. There is a high sense of security that comes with being totally protected and being attached to a God that owns everything. The fact that God sent His son to die for their sins makes them feel more unique and successful. By Jesus' death, plus resurrection, and their willingness to be successful, these individuals took an advantage of a valuable opportunity. The bold act of believing Jesus and accepting Him as their personal savior secured them a right in God's kingdom as children of the Creator. This is powerful. No wonder these Christians were quick in their responses. Moreover, joy and confidence were evident in the tone of their voice. I found a similarity with these Christians' relationship with God and my relationship with my children. My children do not worry about what to eat, drink, wear, and other needs because they trust that dad will deliver. As a father on the other hand, I expect my children to obey my instructions and be generally good. The mere knowledge of the fact that their needs will be satisfied, serves as an incentive or a motivator for my children to obey. Obedience draws rewards. So, if you have tried a lot of things and still don't feel successful, I suggest you try what these Christians have tried.

I have a quote that   supports my analysis. It goes this way: "Master your relationship with the One who owns everything before mastering everything that He owns".

Another outstanding fact in my observation is that if you give people what they are looking for, they are very likely to remain with you or come back even if they leave. For example, a supervisor that I know personally, who has worked more than 20 years in a manufacturing plant told me that the reason that he has simply resisted the temptation to leave his present job is because of the company's retirement program. He even told me that he does not contribute anything towards his 401(K) retirement program. He confided in me that he thinks that the attractive retirement program is the plant's secret for keeping employees for such a long time. Some have retired and still came back to work part-time for the company.

Similarly, I have consistently visited one car mechanic shop for more than 7 years. The owner is honest with pricing and takes pride in his work. Success for him is each time a person leaves his shop satisfied. His style draws back his customers and consequently assures a steady growth of his treasury.

These annotations in the last two paragraphs, in a way, agree with two of my quotes listed in the last chapter. "Give your treasured employees, partners, or clients what they cannot find elsewhere and they will remain with you." "I'm back because you were reliable the last time"

Another important point in my research is that I could not find two people who have exactly the same definition for success. The main theme of this book is to help us define success meaningfully by sharing other people's experiences and ideas relative to success.

God will bless you as much as you want to succeed meaningfully. I have shared again, and I still believe sharing transcends all aspects of love.

Chapter 3

PLANNING FOR EXELLENCE

I will begin this chapter by defining *plan*. Your plan is your blueprint, your design, your layout, your map, your proposition, your representation, your schedule, and your strategy. Your plan actually explains where you have been, where you are, where you are going, and how to get to your destination.

I strongly believe that individuals and businesses must have a plan. Plan is an essential navigation tool. A plan should be genuine, and actually reflect how an entity is doing now, and at the same time, project a more prosperous image.

Based on what is going on in the 21st century, I discourage planning to succeed regardless of who gets crushed. As a result, the first step *should be rooting yourself or business in God*. Just be good and don't worry about it. "The righteous is more excellent," Proverbs 12:26 says. I have my own quotes in regards to this: " Success without God is a sure mess." God gave me this quote one Saturday morning, and I woke up to write it down so that I can share it with my friends, readers, and family. You can find more like this in the last chapter.

On May 11, 2004, I was not really surprised when the directors of Dixie Loan Mortgage Incorporated called me for some business updates, but more important is the dedication of their newly expanded business site to God. No wonder their business is expanding even in a bad economy. We thanked God together, prayed together, and talked business together. In the end, they assured me that their business will continue to function as fairly as possible and according to the word of God.

In Psalms 32:8, God unambiguously indicated that "I will instruct thee and teach thee in the way which thou shall go: I will guide thee with mine eyes." This verse will make more sense when you try to align it with my definition of plan.

In Proverbs 3: 5-7, the Bible went further to tell us to "Trust in the Lord with all thine heart; and lean not unto thine own understanding: In all thy ways acknowledge Him, and He shall direct thy path. Be not wise in thine own eyes: fear the Lord and depart from evil."

The word of God declares in Proverbs that the fear of the Lord is the beginning of wisdom and the knowledge of Him is understanding. It is pertinent to make reference again to my definitions and assimilate them together.

Proverbs 13:11, "He that gathereth by labour shall increase", encourages us to work hard. Hard work is the only route to success and satisfaction regardless of what realm we are dealing with. Naturally, humans are actually meant to climb or walk and not fly. If humans were inescapably made to fly, God would have equipped us accordingly. These lines actually support the fact that success at whatever you want, takes time, patience, and whatever practice a person needs in order to master the positive forces responsible for his or her satisfaction.

Like I mentioned earlier, based on my survey, people that actually love God tend to be more successful. The spiritual minded people that I talked to have a fair and simple perspective of what success means to them. I believe that the relationship that they have with a God that knows and owns everything instilled a high degree of confidence. Such assurance enhances the growth of other aspects of their lives. Such assertion, simplifies the meaning of success to them. This sort of credence has led to the exclusion of some ungodly and expensive behaviors from their plan. On the other hand, such acceptance has resulted in the insertion of Godly and rewarding factors in their plan. If these additions are done well, the outcome is nothing but extreme success in the natural and spiritual realms. For example, an individual, man/woman, whose financial statement reveals a positive net worth, based on the inclusion of some high-quality ingredients in his or her family plan, is considered an extremely successful and reputable leader. I chose to use adjectives like 'extremely' and 'exceedingly' to qualify this type of achievement because I have experienced regular success and extreme success. An individual or business is extraordinarily successful because exceeding joy and happiness are stuffed in the achievement. You will identify extreme success by the degree of joy and happiness attached to such accomplishment.

Some thinkers may question your success if you are a CEO or a president of a well-managed corporation or a head of a financially sound organization whose family's net-worth is constantly depicted in negative. Many have not come to the realization that it takes great management skills to run a family, too. The same principles that apply to running an organization, apply to running a family. You do not want your expenses to exceed your income. I tell my family this all the time. You also want your assets to outweigh your liabilities. Goals have to be met. Human resources, as well as, financial resources have to be nurtured to grow. The family has to believe in something or everything will distract the family.

As a result of the above demands, I recommend that families get a plan that includes periodical budgeting so that they do not live above their income. Tremendous savings can come by way of excluding unnecessary competition with a family that you do not actually know what their income and expense level look like. Shop where you can afford, and not where you think will elevate your status in the community. You do not necessarily have to purchase a commodity simply because it is more expensive than a rival. An expensive item may turn out to be of a poorer quality than a less expensive item. There is nothing wrong with buying affordable brand-name goods. The only point that I am trying to make is that you have to use the situational approach to management in determining when your budget allows you to spend on such goods. You ordinarily don't want to spend outside your budget just to fit in or to feed a peer pressure.   In my opinion, there is something wrong with charging $230 on you credit card for your son or daughter's brand name tennis shoes. The fact that you purchased it with a credit card may be a signal of a purchase made outside a budget.

"Money could be saved on brand-name clothing if you shop at their outlets and if you pay attention to the sales racks at department stores." Julie Simmons, a wealth management executive, concurred.

If you are interested in quality, spend time and read the component statement or labels of the product. If you are interested in buying according to your budget, make that choice yourself. Don't let a reputation or a standard set by your community eat deep into your family's happiness. In the end, what counts is your net worth. Some of us do not know that banks or other financial institutions may want to ascertain the value of your family's net worth when processing your loan or refinancing your projects. Your net worth is simply determined by subtracting your liabilities from your assets. So if you have a kind of plan, you should make some assumptions, ascertain your standing, before even talking to a bank.

Some habits can eat into your family's asset. Unfortunately, some of these habits have double-creased negative impacts. By this, I mean that they will cost you unnecessary money, and at the same time, degrade your health. Such addictive behaviors include, but are not limited to, cigarette smoking, expensive liquor drinking, and gambling adventures. These negatives are very expensive, and without a budget one does not realize how much these factors steal from his or her family's treasury. Tobacco has become a billion-dollar industry because of the overwhelming support gained from consumers. Worthy of inclusion in your plan that, in actual fact, deserve mention are paying your tithes, giving your offerings, and sharing with people or sowing a seed. Your harvest becomes even multiplied when the recipients pay tithe on the gift that you gave them. The author calls this a *reproduction effect theory*. I have experienced an immense amount of benefits from utilizing this theory. When my mother was alive, she paid tithes on money that I gave her. My sisters do the same. One who refuses to be a practitioner of these positives should not be envious at a practitioner's favor from God, in response to being obedient. The Bible tells me that there is much treasure in the house of the righteous but in the revenues of the wicked is trouble.

God said, "Because he hath seth his love upon Me, therefore will I deliver him. I will set him on high, because he hath known my Name. He shall call upon me, and I will answer him: I will be with him in trouble: I will deliver him and honor him." This particular quotation reminds me of a folklore my father used to tell me when he wanted to encourage me to run some errands for him. My father summarized the story by saying that a turtle told his son this: "If you make me happy, I will make you happy in return."

I believe that a person has to be asinine to exempt himself or herself from such a covenant.

After all, it is a known fact that in some parts of the world today, cults require people to sacrifice and kill their blood relatives so that their business will blossom and consequently they will become rich and well known in the community. This is a very detrimental addition to anybody's plan. My own Bible tells me that wealth gotten by vanity shall be diminished, but that gathereth by labor shall increase. No wonder such evil wealth ends in catastrophe. This doesn't necessarily imply that any wealth that decreases is rooted in evil foundation. God may have His own plan for you.

It is realistic to note at his point that being a Christian or Spirit-filled will not guarantee a complete trouble-free business. The devil and his apostles will come to persecute you simply because you built your business on Christian principles. The difference here is that God has promised to interfere. What an incentive to root your business or personal plan on God.

Let us now go to the second step in my recommendation, which is the *rationale for plan*.

You may need a plan just to serve as a directive. You need a map-like instrument to show you where you used to be, where you are now, and where you are going. For an individual, your Bible should serve as your directive. In addition to your Bible, you should be humble, you should be obedient to God's instructions, and you should pay close attention to your parent's teaching, your pastor's instructions, your prophet's directions, and a good mentor's advice. Your ability to master the relationship with the things around you, with the people around you, and with God will unequivocally make obvious to you where you are now, where you are going, and where you used to be. If you are a business entity, there are no two ways. You definitely need a written business plan.

Business Plan

If you are a start up business, it requires money to function. Even if you are an existing business, it takes money to develop. In both cases, you may need funds for your business, and if you do, a business plan is a requirement. You will clearly explain how the money that you are asking for will grow your company and yield profit, which is the reason for going into business. Every lender will want to ascertain how they can get their money back.

Do a thorough analysis of the business you are going into if you are a start up. Research and study hard if you do not have the necessary background for entry level in the business.

Worthy of mention is the fact that people spend money or time on business plan before taking care of their credit standing. I do not recommend borrowing with your credit card to start business like some consultants or web sites counsel. One thing that these advisors do not state is the high charges that come with credit card transactions. You may want to get funds from personal savings, close associates, close friends, or family. Your family member may sympathize with your past financial catastrophe, but it is important to know that all financial institutions will look at your credit history. My personal advice at this point is for a person to make necessary arrangements relative to paying his/her debt before embarking on another borrowing. I believe that you have to show your ability to manage debt. You really have to know that your integrity is at stake here. You have to show that you are a good person to do business with. Also you have to demonstrate that what you are seeking will be in good hands and consequently result in profit. Remember, he that diligently seeks good procureth favor.

I also advise people to build some investment like savings, Certificate of Deposit (CD), land, and house if they have the opportunity. I know some investment associates that will help you when you are ready. While these factors may not be requirements, you are looking at factors that come into play when a financial institution starts looking at your plan, your worth, and your request for a loan.

If you are new in the business or starting, I encourage you to first take care of the sources of funds and their requirements before acquiring many other resources like human resources because it will take money to pay for these resources. Effective planning entails having things in order of priority.

There are many available options for securing capital depending on your suitability. You may want to tap on your personal savings if you have it   This also depends on the size of your business venture. The fact that you are sponsoring your own business does not exclude you from having a business plan. At this stage, the plan will serve as a map or a directive needed to guide you throughout the existence of your business. It will help you to evaluate and make determinations relative to being profitable. The plan will be telling you where you were yesterday, where you are today, and where you are heading tomorrow. Your business may be heading towards enormous expansion, which requires enormous financing. If you already have an organized and a well-written plan, you'll be at an advantage.

Another option is gathering friends or family members who can deliver. Still you have to show them why they should entrust you with such a large amount.

A viable option is seeking the service of a financial institution or agencies like **Small Business Administration (SBA)**, which guarantees loans and has intermediary lenders. The United States Congress mandated the Small Business Administration to help small businesses in accomplishing their goals financially. The agency guarantees loans to small businesses.

According to Small Business Administration (SBA), some of their programs include the MicroLoan program and the Loan Guaranty program. The 7(a) MicroLoan program provides loans up to $25,000. The loan will come from an SBA intermediary lender.

On the 7(a) Loan guaranty program, the SBA guarantees loans up to $750, 000. As the name of this program suggests, SBA assures a lender that the government will pay in case the business cannot pay. The government pays up to the amount guaranteed. The SBA can guarantee 80% on loans up to $100,00 and 75% on loans greater than $100,000.

Like I discussed earlier, these loans will not just be thrown at you. You have to bring something to the table. You have to bring a well-written business plan. Also, you have to show through your past business transactions that you are a reliable individual. You have to present a management team that could be entrusted with such a large sum.

There are more programs available with SBA. I believe SBA will be in a better position to discuss the requirements for each program.

The SBA has offices all over the United States. If you need more help, call 1-800-827-5722 for information on the nearest SBA office. Just Try.

If you intend to open a farming business, you may want to check with the United States Department of Agriculture, **Farm Service Agency (FSA)** which will guarantee your loan.

Regardless of which party you seek out for funds, you must be ready with your plan to illustrate that the goods or services you provide have the potential of being successful. It may be necessary to have in your plan, results of research done on behalf of your business. More so, you can ask people who have benefited from your goods or services to write some recommendations, which can be affixed to your plan.

61

If you are already in the business, you will have to show profitability through a basic income statement that will describe your income and expense. You may be required to present a balance sheet, which will list your assets and equities. These statements will depict how beneficial or dangerous it is to do business with you. I support the inclusion of "Executive Summary" in your business plan. Some people overlook this but the executive summary, as the name suggests, is your plan summarized in a shorter form. My rationale for supporting the inclusion of executive plan is that some financial institutions' executives who may not have time to go through your voluminous plan may find reasonable cause by just glancing at the summary. Consequently, a well-written executive plan is valuable.

Another factor worthy of a space in your plan, in order to prove that you have the potential for success is the location of your business. You will have to show that your business is strategically located and has a competitive edge over similar existing businesses. Do not just locate anywhere simply because the cost is affordable. Search for a location that has enough traffic flow, has enough parking spaces, has less crime, and is easily accessible.

Get your management team together. This is an interesting area to most lenders. Financial institutions will like to know the management team. Your plan has to show that the business is going to be managed to the point of profitability. Select a team of managers who will help you to project your goals positively, years in advance, and give room for competent evaluation and reassessment of your plan if changes are needed. These changes could result from anticipated and unanticipated impacts, ranging from financial to human resources.

Family Budget Planning

I consider a family as a business entity. I manage my family's resources like every other business manager would. Like a business, you may want to keep financial statements. Your family's wealth should be graded by your net worth and not your income. This is simply a statement that tells you if you are spending wisely or not, compared to the family's income. A family planner should be able to distinguish between a liability and asset. The family leader should plan for his children's future. Don't procrastinate, hoping to be a millionaire before investing in your family's future.

Dependent upon how your territory is being enlarged, you may need a standardized balance sheet and an income statement some day. A balance sheet is nothing more than a financial record that explains your assets, liabilities, and net worth in a particular period. Remember that your assets are those things that belong to you that can be turned into money. Your liabilities are all those debts that you owe. Your net worth is determined by subtracting your liabilities from your assets. The result could be either positive or negative. A positive result means that you are doing well, but a negative result is an indication that your liabilities are more than you should have.

How to Increase Your Family's Net Worth

There are so many approaches to managing your family's resources and consequently save and elevate your net worth. Let us review some, but if have more questions, you can contact my consulting firm.

Budgeting

The first thing that you have to do is to start budgeting. Your budget is a plan of income and expense or a plan of revenue and expenditure. If you don't have one, just start one as soon as you get through reading this book. Just get a sheet of paper and start writing down your income and expense for the month making sure that the projected expenses do not exceed your projected income. I will suggest that you categorize your expenses. For example, vehicle expenses, mortgage expenses, utility expenses, grocery expenses, outfit expenses, church expenses, etc, and savings.

Evaluate your Plans Periodically

If the end of the month's evaluation indicates that you are spending more on any category of expense than your mortgage, this may signal a problem, and then you should reassess your plan. No other category should absorb more than your mortgage. I have an exception here. Unless you are doubling your payment on an item like a car, wanting to pay it off with the realization that vehicle depreciates in value as time goes by.

Start Buying a House if You Can

House or land is one of the greatest assets a family can have. If you do not have the necessary resources needed to acquire a house now, probably due to too much debt, have patience, pay off the unnecessary debts, and work towards getting a house. Besides the fact that the value of your house goes up, the interest on mortgage payment is tax deductible. You cannot go wrong.

Family Assistance: USDA (Rural Development) has a program that helps people in certain areas or rural cities obtain a house loan. According to USDA, this Direct Homeownership Loan program allows you to make payment based on income. You have to show inability to obtain homeownership loan from a bank or other financial institution.

You pay interest as low as 1% and no down payment is required. This loan is designated for families whose income and credit will not allow them to obtain a conventional loan. According to

USDA, it is estimated that approximately $54 billion has been invested in this venture to help people buy or build their own homes. I don't see what you have to loose by trying. Pray, pick up the phone, and dial (202) 720-4323 and press #1 and that will connect you to your Rural Development State Office.

Even if your income is very high to qualify for a direct loan, USDA Rural Development may guarantee your loan made by banks or other financial institutions. This guarantee allows lenders to lend money to individuals that they will not otherwise have lent money because of income or credit problems. The USDA Rural Development may expect your income to be below 115% of the area income. You will be better off contacting your Rural Development Office instead of trying to figure out if you are qualified. They are the specialists in that area and I believe they will work with you.

Refinance If Possible

If you already have a house, and the mortgage is financed for 30 years, you can save your family a lot of money if you refinance it to a lower number of years, preferably 15. This point is particularly true if the interest rate falls below certain percentage. Get with your bank, management, or financial consultant for more information. Furthermore, I suggest that you do not fall into the trap of adjustable rate over fixed rates. These terms can be confusing, particularly for those of you who have not bought a house before. The difference here is that the fixed rate will not fluctuate. By this I mean that it will not go up or down.

Increase Payment on Principal

Depending on your family's financial standing, you can add something every time you make a payment. This not only shortens the length of your payment, it builds equity. You have to apply the contingency approach to management here, which requires management action based on your family's financial situation and available resources.

Savings on Telephone Bills

The family manager should always look at himself or herself as a manager of a business entity. You want to make profit by way of all reasonable savings. If, for example, you think that your family spends a lot of money making long distance telephone calls, you can discipline yourself by buying phone cards with time and price already affixed to it. On the other hand, you can make effective use of your electronic mail (e–mail). I practice the last option, depending on the type of feedback I want from the recipient of my information. More important, you should contact your telephone carrier for up-to-date information on specials. For example, Bellsouth has plans that include, but not limited to, unlimited long distance plan, and Complete Choice plan. Bellsouth even has a low-income assistance plan for home telephone service. If you have someone that receives Medicaid benefits, he or she may be qualified for such assistance. Similarly, AT&T and other carriers have plans that will help you customize according to your own plan. The major advantage of these plans from a budgeting perspective is that you will pretty much know what your bill will look like every month

Go For Retirement Plans

Sound retirement plans increase savings. It definitely grows your net worth. If you work for a company that offers 401(K) or similar plans, you should take advantage of such retirement programs. You can put in as much as your present financial situation allows. There are enormous advantages of having such a retirement plan. First, most employers match these funds. Second, contribution is deducted before tax and that saves you some tax money. Third, your company always hands your contribution to financial experts who manage your money based on what fund you choose and the percentage of money allocated to your desired investment. You have the responsibility of choosing how the administrator should invest your money.

Traditional IRA and Roth IRA

IRA is an undisputable tax-advantaged investment for your personal retirement fund.

There are two types of IRA, the Traditional and Roth IRA. U.S. Congress has made IRAs available for anyone who earns income. The good parts about IRA are that your contributions are tax-deductible and growth is tax-deferred.

Traditional IRA

If you are under 70½ years old, work full time or part time, you are eligible for the Traditional IRA. You may be allowed to open a Traditional IRA regardless of your level of income. There are two advantages that a person gains by opening a Traditional IRA.

· 1st advantage- Tax deductible: You may be allowed to deduct part or all contributions on you income tax.

· 2nd advantage- Tax-deferred: The growth in your IRA is tax-deferred. This simply means that you do not have to pay federal taxes on the earnings, until you start to withdraw money from IRA. I think this sounds great. You can start withdrawing your money without any sort of penalty as soon as you turn 59½. But if you decide to withdraw your money before age 59½, your money may be subjected to 10% tax.

Also, you are allowed to open an IRA from January 1st through the deadline for filing federal income tax return. This is normally around April 15 of each year.

Roth IRA

The Congress created the Roth IRA as part of the Taxpayer Relief Act of 1997. As the name suggests, it was named after a former U.S. Senator, William Roth. The good part of Roth IRA is that the growth of your assets could be tax-free. You may not pay a federal income tax when you withdraw your assets. For example, if you are using your withdrawal as a first time house purchaser, you will not pay any federal taxes.

Also, unlike the Traditional IRA, you do not have to be under age 70½ to participate. Anyone, regardless of your age, can get involved. I am not going to wait until I'm 120 years old before I start investing in the Roth IRA.

Another attraction is the fact that if you reach 59½ years old, and have had your Roth IRA for five years, you can withdraw your money without paying income tax. If you die or become disabled at or after 59½ years old, you also will receive your money without paying federal income tax. Even if you're not disabled, did not satisfy the requirements for first-time house buyer, or have not had the Roth IRA for at least 5 years, just the growth part of your Roth IRA will be taxed based on 10% penalty.

Both Traditional and Roth IRAs are great investments, but you may have to make your choice based on the information given and what will result to personal satisfaction.

Pay Your Debts As Agreed

Always try to pay your bills as agreed. If for any reason you cannot pay on time, contact the people that you owe and arrange a payment plan. You do not want to jeopardize your credit rating to the point that you will become a candidate for high percentage interest rates. There is definitely a difference between a person paying at a 5% rate and another paying at a 20% rate. For the former it is a savings and for the latter, it is mismanagement at its best.

Compare Your Credit Card Account & Your Savings Account

If you have a credit card balance of, let's say, $5000 .00 to pay and a savings account balance of $5000.00, I suggest that you compare the interest that the bank is paying you with interest rate, finance charges, and what ever you pay monthly. I intend not to disclose the outcome because I want my clients/readers to practically do this plain evaluation. Consequently, I expect a sound judgment on your part. As a matter of fact, I have two credit cards as at the time I am writing this book, but thank God both have a zero balance. It is nothing personal against credit card companies. I just have to look out for my self/family.

Children/Human Resources

You should treat your children just like an effective employer will treat his human resources. Remember, your human resources are the most important of all your resources. Get your children fully involved in your plan. Educate them on the forms of relevant spending. Make them aware of the consequences of deviating from set standards.

You should incorporate motivational or incentive packages in your plan. Every family's income and budget differs, so it will be wrong for me to advise a family on what to do without knowing the family's financial standing. I use things as little as shopping and going out to eat as incentive packages relevant to behaviors that will increase savings for the family.

You will be surprised how much these children will work hard to make sure that the family's goals and objectives are met.

Invest in Your Children's Future

Investing in your children's education is one of the best things you can do for your children. The 529 plan is great because it offers tax-free withdrawal for college related costs. Also, the growth on your contribution is tax deferred. If you think that your child or children will qualify for financial aid, you may have to invest more carefully at your own pace without pressuring your family financially. If you cannot afford to pay for the services of a financial consultant at this point in your life, you can take a conservative approach and do it little by little.

You can consider investing in **U.S. Savings Bond**. I have been investing in U.S. Savings Bond for more than 10 years. The good parts about U. S. Saving Bonds are that you don't have to pay state or local tax on interest earned. The market rates of U. S. Bonds are adjusted every six months in order to remain competitive. If you use your bonds to pay for college tuition, you may even qualify to pay no federal tax on interest that you earned. The contribution is backed by U. S. Government. You can purchase as little as $25.00 for a $50.00 bond. That was how I got started. You can redeem your bond in about six months without getting the full face value. In order to get your full face value, you will have to wait for 17 years. Moreover, you earn interest on these bonds and if the interest rates are high, you may be able to reach your face value even before your maximum 17 years. I don't pay any fees to purchase my bonds. Furthermore, I don't have to worry about it as much as my stocks because it is protected by the federal government and you pretty much can tell what you're getting/keeping compared to stocks, which fluctuates a great deal, and which may, in most cases, require an expert advice of a stock broker. I have invested in stocks for over 12 years. Almost all my stocks are invested under Dividend Reinvestment Plan (DRP). I like well-managed food and utility companies. I am basically growth oriented when it comes to stock investment. I am not even talking about aggressive growth here. My main objective is to look for appreciation in the worth of my asset.

Coverdell Education Savings Accounts

With the steadily increasing tuition, room and board, U.S. Congress created this account to help families prepare for college expenses. This account is specifically created for education. It is not a retirement investment.

What makes this account extremely attractive is the fact that it offers tax-deferred growth and tax-free withdrawals.

Please note that the contributions to Coverdell Education Savings Account are never tax-deductible. But if you withdraw money to pay for tuition, room, board, books, or other school expenses, such withdrawal is tax-free.

In my own opinion, this account is a great vehicle for accumulating towards your child or children's educational expenses, particularly if you are certain that your child will not qualify for financial aid.

Increase Savings by Buying Government Inspected Meat Food Products

You can save a lot of money on medical bills by buying meat or food products inspected by the appropriate government agency designated to do so. It is not illegal for you to slaughter and prepare a livestock of your own raising for consumption with your family, guests, or employees. It may be illegal for you to distribute and sell without state or federal permission. Please do not fall into the trap of buying meat products that are not inspected from unregulated sellers. Their products may be cheaper today, but may cost you a lot tomorrow. It could cause you emotional and financial trauma. There are many pathogenic organisms (capable of causing illness) associated with meat/poultry food products that an unregulated source is not properly equipped to prevent or eliminate. For example, Salmonella can cause sudden headache, abdominal pain, fever, dehydration caused by diarrhea, vomiting, or even death, particularly to the elderly and children. Similarly, Listeria Monocytogen can cause severe illness like fever, headache, vomiting, or even death. Furthermore, E-coli can cause dehydration, diarrhea, or even kidney problem. There are many more of these pathogens, but the good news here is that the government has well trained inspectors with up-to-date programs necessary for the prevention and eradication of these organism before they can get to the consumers and steal from them physically and financially. Today's purchase of government inspected meat/food products is tomorrow's savings on medical bills.

Give to Charitable Organizations & Save

Here is another instance where you have to exclude the unwanted and include the needed. The money you spend on most charitable organizations or other church related activities is tax deductible and accountable on earth and in Heaven. On the other hand, the money spent on gambling, buying cigarettes, and expensive alcohol is not tax deductible and not recorded in Heaven.

From a budgeting point of view, the savings on these factors can mean a substantial current asset relative to your family's net worth. For example, at the time that this book was written, Chicago area had a tax increase of 82-cent-per-pack, bringing the per pack cost to about $6.00. In New York, the cost of cigarette is about $7.00. For a family that smokes two packs a day, you are looking at $5,110.00 a year. For some families, it costs about the same amount to satisfy their alcohol wants. So you are looking at $10,000 or more annually for these two. I have saved a lot of money since I excluded the large bottle of *red rose wine,* from our grocery list, and included *pure water*, *sparkling juice*, and non-alcoholic *Spumante fre.*

From an increase perspective, you will save thousands of dollars directly and indirectly at the end of the year. The direct savings will come by way of not spending on these habits. The indirect savings will come by way of not paying expensive hospital bills for sicknesses related to the habits.

Also, your tithes, offerings, and other seeds sown have bi-directional benefits. You may deduct them from your income tax (consult your tax advisor about the deductibility) and still receive the blessings that come with having a Heavenly account.

Positive Net Worth

The key, or the bottom line for you and me, is having a positive net worth at the end of a period. Be it a day, a month, or a quarter. Make sure that your liabilities are not greater than your assets. It is very advantageous to accumulate those subjects that will appear on the asset column of your financial statements than to accumulate those factors that will appear on the liability column of your financial statement. Just knowing this basic financial planning will take you and your family a long way. Enjoy God's promise.

The following chart helps you in making decisions on how to apply your financial resources positively. You should never determine your wealth based on your income. It should be based on your net worth. This financial statement should serve as your guide in ascertaining your financial standing. Based on this information, you can make adjustments in reference to your investing and spending strategies.

The Praiser U. Tither Family

Family Income (annual)...................$102,000

ASSETS

Savings......................................10,200
Vested Interest Retirement Funds.......26,000
Market Value of Home....................46,000
Stocks......................................3,300
Checking....................................1,200
E. E. Bonds.................................1,050

Total.. ....$87,750

LIABILITIES

Auto Loan.................................$28,000
Student Loan.................................3,000
Other Loans 2,600
Total other debts............................1,800
Credit Cards 500
Mortgage Payable............................8,760

Total.. ....$44,660

Net Worth $43,090

---

*This financial statement is just an illustration. None of these figures depict the real financial standing for the Praiser U. Tither family.

     I will conclude this chapter with this affirmation. The above-discussed planning factors will certainly increase your business or family's net worth and materially make you successful.

Unfortunately, *extreme success* as I write about it, is not only about being materially rich. You have what I call *"an unsuccessful rich"* and *"a success with reduced finance"*. *An unsuccessful rich person* does not really share his/her wealth, does not have a good relationship with God and human, does not have love in his/her heart, and is not really happy. But on the other hand, *a success with reduced finance,* may not be loaded with cash, but has the above characteristics and, is not selfish.

A very successful businesswoman named Vera once told me, "Success for me is when I can make a difference with what I have. I don't mind giving 99% of what I have towards helping others. This makes me happy."

I know another very successful professional named Rita who kept asking God to bless her with more than enough so that she can share. God gave her a little, which she shared, and abundance coupled with happiness followed.

In 2001, I received a gift from a lady that I consider *a success with reduced finance.* She shared with the little she had. It brought tears to my eyes but I held myself. Do you know what? Her financial condition has dramatically changed as of this writing. Her river is gradually turning into an ocean with varieties therein.

CHAPTER 4

MARKETING FOR EXCELLENCE

Your marketing involves those things that you have to do to influence, and find out how your products and services will satisfy customers' needs and wants.

What I encourage my clients/readers to do is stick with the truth when advertising. Believe in yourself, your management team, and your product.

Promotion and advertising are the most influential forces in getting the attention of your buyers or potential buyers. Both are essential ingredients to your profitability.

You have to use your promotion in persuading your customers. Your message or choice of medium for promotion has to be credible.

If you have not grown to the point of having a department in your company designated to do your advertising, you can choose an advertising agency. If you cannot afford an advertising agency at this point, you can choose affordable media like newspapers, church bulletin, consumer magazines, business cards, and fliers. Research has proved that these methods are very reliable.

It is my honest suggestion that you use simple and easy to understand expressions. Tell your potential customers or current customers about your product to the best of your ability. Describe your product so favorably in a way that a rival product will distinguishably look somewhat inferior. Stay away from making or drumming up unfounded stories about your product.

If you adhere to the truth you will not be entrapped by regulatory laws, which most people are ignorant or unaware of. What sellers say about their products is regulated. The Federal Trade Commission (FTC) has the power to bring a proceeding in order to question a marketing style considered deceptive or unfair.

Also, qualities of products are regulated by the Consumer Product Safety Commission (CPSC). They are responsible in making sure that consumer products are safe.

The Food and Drug Administration (FDA) regulates how you make and sell your food, drug, and cosmetics.

The United States Department of Agriculture (USDA) regulates how meat, poultry, and egg products are made and sold. They make sure that the consumers get exactly what the product claims on the packages and other methods of advertising. You cannot include in your advertisement what you do not have in the product. Your advertising is false or deceptive if it has information or does not have information that is likely to mislead. There are inspectors assigned in each establishment by the government to make sure that consumers' interests are protected.

There are numerous regulatory institutions, but they differ depending on what you produce and sell. But the bottom line is being truthful about what you are producing and marketing. Failure to pay attention to this fact may result to an expensive fine or lawsuit that may knock you out of business. So be careful.

Always do a thorough research before choosing a medium of promotion. Have a clear understanding of whom you are trying to reach. This will tell you what method to pursue. Some of the factors that influence advertisement are ages of the buyers, sex of the buyers, income of the buyers, educational level of the buyers, and the season of the year (Is the product you are intensively advertising suited for that particular weather?).

For example, if you are trying to reach children, using the newspaper may not be your best option. If you are selling what everybody wants, a time that a television program that is designed for everybody is airing is the best time to schedule for your commercial.

My teenage daughters always enjoy reading magazines like *Seventeen*, Your *Magazine (YM)*, and *Teen Vogue*. The only way I can effectively reach my daughters and their friends is by advertising in such magazines' designed for teenagers. Some Christian based magazines that may serve, as good sources of advertising are *Refuel* and *Revolve*. *Refuel* is a Christian teen magazine for guys while *Revolve* is a Christian teen magazine for girls.

On the other hand, my sons, who are young children, watch a lot of children's TV programs.

The only method of getting their attention is having a colorful and exciting commercial that is shown during the time that children watch television.

In some cases, selling requires a person-to-person interaction. You may want to reach a group that does not read, watch television, or listen to the radio regularly.

Personal Selling

Sometimes you may want to be present to answer questions and convince a potential consumer of the importance of your product. Before embarking on personal selling, train or choose sales people that have strong knowledge of the products, sales people that are, not biased but, willing to answer customers questions objectively, sales people that have confidence in themselves and in the products that they are selling, sales people who are persistent, sales people who are people-oriented, and sales people who do not have problem following up to make sure that their customers are utterly satisfied.

Pricing

You must price your goods and services properly in order to be profitable. If there are similar businesses or services already in existence in the same area before you, I suggest that you use a sort of market penetration. Market penetration is a sort of strategy that allows you to slightly lower your price so that you can have a customer base. But regardless of what method used, remember that you are in the business to make profit. Lowering prices initially should never come at the expense of total cost. It should not compromise profit. Your price should be able to absorb the cost of your production. This cost involves everything that you spend before the product enters in the hand of your customer. This is one of the reasons that it is important to plan and manage your resources efficiently so that the cost of producing the product will not be so much that you will be forced to price yourself out of competition.

Always remember that all your marketing or promotional activities are considered operating expenses. In order to get a *net profit*, you will subtract your operating expenses from gross income. Furthermore, you will have to subtract your cost of goods from sales of goods in order to get your *gross profit*. You have to differentiate between how much a product costs you, and how much you sold it.

Online Selling

I am not an expert on web design, but one thing is certain, we all know that your website serves as a promotional or marketing weapon, too. Get an individual who actually knows about website design so that potential or ready costumers will frequently visit your site. In the 21st century, website is an essential selling tool. Your website ad should have the necessary designs to portray your product adequately. Foods are some of the products that demand color amalgamation when advertising on television or on the Internet. On the other hand, the advertisement of a CD, audiocassette, etc. will need sufficient sound management. Your designer should know enough about search engines so that your registration on a particular engine will ensure proper traffic flow.

Chapter 5

ACCOUNTING FOR EXCELLENCE

This chapter is not written for upper echelon accountants or financial managers. Rather it is put together for men and women (business or non business) who must know the basic terms in order to comprehend few of the things that these accountants and other financial experts are saying. I believe that a business owner, a potential business owner, or a manager should be able to look at a financial statement and have a basic understanding of the meanings of frequently used terms in financial statements.

The accountants that I do business with do not charge their clients fees for counseling. We will be glad to hook you up with these accountants if you contact my business firm. If you already have an accountant, don't be afraid to call them on questions concerning your financial standing. While a busy accountant may go straight to the core of your financial status, he or she may not have the time to teach you basic accounting or financial terms pertinent to the ultimate comprehension of your financial status. So if you equip yourself with this book and its valuable contents, you will be ready for most transactions. You will be doing yourself a favor by learning these terms on your own. The complete understanding of these basics will enhance the excellence that you are pursuing in your business.

I have not met one personally, but I have heard about some millionaires who got broke because of their inability to understand basic financial terms.

I assure you that if you begin to gradually internalize these terms, the intimidation that comes with some of these financial records will no longer have a place in you.

ASSETS--Those things that you own that have a positive cash value.

CURRENT ASSETS--Those particular assets that you can turn into cash in no more than one year. Examples of current assets are cash, account receivable, merchandise inventories, short-term investments, and prepaid expenses.

CASH--Money that belongs to you. It could be physical dollars or checking account.

ACCOUNT RECEIVABLE--Money owed to you from normal operation of business.

MERCHANDISE INVENTORY--These are goods like raw materials or goods bought for resale that has not been sold.

SHORT-TERM INVESTMENTS--These are investments like CDs, stocks, and bonds that are meant to be turned into cash in about a year.

PREPAID EXPENSES--Goods or services that you spent on before use. Things that fall into this category are usually insurance, rent, or deposit.

FIXED ASSETS--These are meaningful resources that are not expected to be resold in the cause of your business operation. Such as land, buildings, furniture, and equipment.

LONG-TERM INVESTMENTS--These are the investments like bonds, stocks, savings that you plan to retain for at least a year. Not less than a year.

LIABILITIES--The debts you owe or the debts that your business owes.

CURRENT LIABILITIES--Debts that have to be paid in less than a year. Such as accounts payable, notes payable, interest payable, and other accrued expenses payable.

ACCOUNTS PAYABLE--the debts that you have to pay within a particular operating circle.

ACCRUED EXPENSES PAYABLE--This could result as a work that I performed, as a consultant, in December of last year, but which has not been paid to me as of the end of last year.

NET WORTH--Is the result you get when you subtract your liabilities from assets. This result could be negative or positive.

BALANCE SHEET--This is that particular financial statement that describes your financial standing at any time or date by listing your assets and liabilities. It is sometimes called a statement of financial position.

INCOME STATEMENT--This is a financial statement that depicts your revenues, expenses, and your profits at a given period of time. It is sometimes called Profit and Loss Statement.

GROSS PROFIT--The result you get when you subtract cost of goods from sales of goods.

NET PROFIT--Result you get when you subtract operation expenses from gross profit.

OWNER'S EQUITY--This is the owner's capital or the owner's claim against a firm's resources. When dealing with corporation it is called Shareholder's Equity.

CASH DIVIDEND—This is the cash that the corporations distribute to their shareholders.

CURRENT RATIO—This is the ratio of current assets to current liabilities. It is simply determined by a formula that has the current assets over the current liabilities.

QUICK RATIO---This is the ratio of current assets inventory to current liabilities. It is simply determined by a formula that has the current assets inventory over liabilities.

For a person to gain a better understanding of those financial statements, it will be pertinent to look at what a simple Income Statement and Balance Sheet look like.

UFAITH CONSULTING SERVICES
Selma, AL
Income Statement
Month Ending April 30, 2004

Sale/Pay for Services Rendered.....	$850
Operating Expenses:	
Salary expense.....................$240	
Supplies expense................... 25	
Advertising expense............... 55	
Depreciation expense.............. 30	
Miscellaneous/other expense...... <u>50</u>	
	400
Net Income..............................	$450

$450 was Ufaith Consulting Services net income for the month ending of April. Remember that an Income Statement also serves as a Profit and Loss Statement, too.

UFAITH CONSULTING SERVICES
Selma, AL
Balance Sheet
Month Ending April 30, 2004

Assets

Current Assets:

Cash..$2000

Accounts Receivable................... 250

Supplies not sold........................ 55

Prepaid Expense........................ 150

Short-Term Investments............... 1000

    Total Current Assets.................. $3455

Fixed Assets:

Equipment................................$2000

    Less accumulated depreciation...... <u>85</u>   <u>1915</u>

Total Assets.................................. <u>$5370</u>

Liabilities

Current Liabilities

Accounts Payable.......................$1000

Miscellaneous/other payables......... 250

Total Liabilities........................... $1250

Net Worth................................   <u>$4120</u>

Ufaith Consulting Services has a positive net worth for $4120, which is good news.

*These two financial statements are just an illustration. None of these figures depict the real financial standing for Ufaith Consulting Services

Chapter 6

QUOTE THE BEST OUT OF YOU
WITH DR. UDO UFOMADU'S
QUOTES & CONCEPTS

A great player covers the mistake
Of a fellow player during a game
But talks it over after the game
Or forgives and forgets about it.

I feel successful when God is happy, when I am
happy, and when my family is happy.

The Ten Commandments is the ultimate instrument
for assessing morality norm.

Success is not tied to luck; It is tied to a promise to
those who diligently
Work hard and seek good.

The mastery of relationship with the Owner of
everything that I want should come first before the
mastery of everything that He owns.

The God of North America is the God of West
Africa; Their harvests are only dependent upon their
seeds, time, and soil.

Be careful whom you elect or choose as a leader, husband, or manager. For a purposeless leader directs a purposeless flock.

Business plan, HAACP plan, personal plan
Are essential navigation tools.

Since I have learned to pray, plan, and wait
for the real Master Planner to initiate the plan. Then
have I harvested more than enough and ate plenty
good through and beyond expected span.

God, the Master Planner, has not failed us yet.

The devil may hate you with a passion.
But you can make him respect you with an action.

If you appreciate a person, he or she will increase in performance.

The Bible is the only reasonable compass for sailing the know-not.

Wisdom without the fear of God is a dangerous wisdom.

Give your treasured employees, partners, or clients what they cannot find elsewhere and they will remain with you.

A wealth of experience awaits you, if you start at
the bottom and grow to the top.

Success without God is on the surface.

A success without the word of God is a sure mess.

Revenge thou not
With a cheaper shot.

Tell not your problems to the people who cannot
solve it or pray genuinely about it.

I am the one that is thirsty,
I am the one that must look for pure water.

We can hope the same way David hoped when he picked up the sling and stone to face Goliath.

Let not a junk immaterialism paralyze
God's favor already delegated to patronize.

Avoid any that's so untrue,
Believe in yourself
As success unwraps itself.

A person that cares
is
A person of the people

You can never become a positive if you
Hear, touch, and meditate in negative.

Not everybody or everything sent to you is designed
for your goodness.
The devil sends some things too.

It is never too late
To achieve and realize
The dreams, goals that await
Attempt, rather than to analyze.

If you show me your mentor/role model,
I will show you what you are likely to become.

A good manager is
That coach who knows how
To get players to play
Together for one purpose.

He that encourages and teaches others,
Encourages and teaches himself too.

Success avenges thy cause.

God formed you to dominate
An awkward, slippery world
That justifies atrocities, injustices
That even great people settle for a compromise.

What you expose your eyes, brain, and ears to
Determine what you seek after and consequently
become.

Let your plans be meaningful,
Moreover, let your goals be attainable.

For you to find something,
You've got to look for it.

106

Your level of obedience
Determines your level of procurement.

Like a beautiful flower
You can blossom
Blossom as a rising star and will shine
Shine more than the brightest stars.

I am going by what God Knew before I was formed
I am not trying to prove anything

Success is designed, arranged, and mapped for them
They that will listen to their parents
Parents that will instill values, take them to a good
church
Church that teaches respect for God, life and
authority.

Love good over malevolence,
Peace and goodness you must like,
Like a beautiful flower,
I know you can blossom.

You may not find what
You are looking for the first time

Because God, the Commander, has
Not disappointed us yet, we must continue
To trust and obey

Not knowing all the answers to my concerns
The succor of the Omniscient was solicited
And He comforted with Psalms 27:1, Psalms 118:6,
Jeremiah 17:5-9, Isaiah 26:4, & Isaiah 41: 10-13.

Her faith fiercely maximized in the right
Capacity, she unequivocally knew that if she may
Touch His cloth; she'd be free of her plight

Your plan and dreams are valueless
Until you implement them.

Always add God to any package
Designated for your children.

The value of your business
Appreciates each time you honestly
Involve God and His principles

Abraham, David, and yourself
Know how bright
It glows when maximized faith turns darkness to
daylight,
That enemies and head enemy when defeated
Resort to flight.

How you do it
Is as important as
How you say it

Faith in God, I have exhibited when I fight
Some battles, yet I crave for faith activated in a way
That all my Goliaths vamoose at my sling's sight.

111

Starting it is the only remedy.

And now my good God, reigning from the greatest height
Show me how to activate, maximize my faith, I pray
So at all times, I'll be one unquenchable, indomitable light.

Your ability should never be
Overshadowed by your inability

You may not be the first to
Think of an idea, but you
May be the first to reap the result
Of putting the idea to action

Your mistakes are regrettable only,
If nothing is learned from it.

To me, a present abode
Is just a palace,
An abode to come is simply a bigger palace.

What ever you call yourself
Is what you really are.

To me a present ride is super,
A ride to come
Is simply a better ride.

Climbing to the top is natural
But flying to the top is unnatural
For wingless creatures.

Real knockout occurs
When you cannot get up again.

To me my family is the best,
A family that fears God
Is simply number one.

Doing what makes you happy
Defines your degree of success

115

To me, my present job is good,
A job to come
Is simply a better job.

How you see it matters less
All I see is enough and excess

To me, I'm just as wealthy
A wealth to come
Is simply an addition

Successful parents instill value
By living the value

"Forwardever" is now a stand nothing will invade

To me, I'm just as healthy,
A health to come
Is a better health.

117

"Was" is the past tense of "is".
If you discover that "was" is not suitable for the
sentence
Don't be afraid to use "is".

Let your ambition
Be on a mission
Faith-backed goals meet you definition
As you embark on a success expedition.

Be aware that discouragement serves prohibition.
Know ye that criticism feeds an inhibition.

Activated confidence and intuition
Will generate a strong acquisition
And diligently attract a coalition
Of honorable and heavenly intervention.

If you know what you
Are looking for, you'll find
What you are looking for.

People strive to be better
When you encourage their effort.

Just peeping through the windows of your heart
I saw the insecurity clouding your eyes
Struggling not to fall apart,
Still you ordinarily fell to rise.

Never let
A bad season
Overshadow
A good season

Nothing is more fulfilling
Than doing what the devil thought
I couldn't do

I know a way out of this pain
Through a God of mercy and love
Waiting and willing to regain
The control of a flier capable as a dove.

The only step I see in front of me is more than
enough.

Achievers always say, " We will try"
And not, "We cannot".

I still reminisce on the last push
Cutting through a deadly ambush
With God, The Master Planner, in the lead
We cut, we fixed, and we reevaluated in full speed.

Why settle for good when best is nigh.

If you keep pretending to be
You'll become.

You are programmed to succeed,
Your little light is still on,
Quench it never.

The first step to solving
A problem is finding out
What the problem is.

The Sauls are running
They head for a change, I hope
The Davids are awake
They head for a victory celebration, I know.

123

The time it takes pretending to conform
Is the same time it will take to conform.
You might as well conform to the norms of the
hopeful.

Goals are now attainable
Even in a packed session of doubters

You can get it
But you must persist
To get it at last

Everybody's ideas are needed
Until they are no longer needed.

For all, the stream of happiness flows
To all the wind of gladness blows
Your choices and your actions make the difference.

There is an Omniscient Consultant that the ordinary
can always share
With the well-to-do & the affluent group of his/her
community;
God is available to all.

125

If you desire to make your vision plain
Make it plain and be happy.

Needless for a man-made god since
The God I serve provides all my needs

If your Christian music
Nourishes your soul,
Nourish you own soul please.

If celebrating in the Lord
Boosts your spirituality,
Boost your spirituality please.

Do not depend on people
To make you happy
Because those people may be unhappy.

If happy gatherings
Satisfy your soul,
Then satisfy your soul.

Remember that your present
Level is a promotion for someone else.

Do not spend all your life
Waiting for someone to advance you.
Promote everything about
Yourself with the wisdom of God.

Wait for no human
To better your life.

Ask questions if you must,
But shut up if you lack
Knowledge on the subject matter being addressed.

Wait for no mortal
Look for positive avenues.

It is better to be a good listener
Than to be considered a foolish talker.

Wait for no mortal
Look for positive avenues.

A friend or relative when things are good,
Should be a friend or relative when things are bad.

Wait for no special rationale
To make yourself happy

Wait and have no doubt
But don't stop praying about it.

Wait no more for their clout,
Have faith and take worthy chance.

Blessed are those who go out of their way
To lessen others burdens.

Wait no longer for your difference to discourage
Turn your uniqueness to assets for all
circumstances.

Give your employer what s/he
Cannot find in someone else and
He will retain you.

Any level of job or education is better
Than having none.

With the Omniscient in our corner to provide
We have got it made

What you teach your children
Is what they will teach your grandchildren

Have you ever thought about
Taking your hobby to the next level?

The portion of your life that you delegate to the
devil
Is the portion that he will work with.

With the Omniscient on the lead to guide
Our conquest has stayed.

A new reaction induces
A new acquisition.

With the Omnipresent now firm on our side
We are confident and unafraid.

If you want new things
Try new things

Backwardness turned a human into a pillar of salt
Looking back endangered and put a travel on a halt.

I'm back because you were reliable the last time.

You have to love something to be good at it.

Playing back kept a loser down
Forward march won the winner a crown.

Some felt I wasn't fit
God called me a perfect fit.

A winner is that individual who
Knows how to fall and get back up,
How to try new things,
And how to persist in good faith.

Some said I couldn't
God said I could.

An effective leader or manager
Learns   what to do, Listens on how to do it,
And helps everybody do it better.

God will reach out to you
The same way you reach out to others.

When tears of sadness
Strolled down
My cheek constantly,
God comforted me immensely.

Wise people know when to tell God
And when to tell man.

When wickedness encompassed
Me for a kill
God lifted me.

When some doubted your capability
God believed in you.

Successful people are not afraid of making mistakes
Rather they avoid making the same mistakes
Over and over.

The Lord is my supplier
There is no rationale for nonsense stress.

When you think hope is gone
God reassures you authoritatively.

Always strive to be better than
Your role model.

If you want to be a leader,
Be willing to learn and be willing to teach,
And be willing to practice what you teach.

How you present yourself
Is how you'll be perceived.

When some saw my cup empty
God called it running over.

The Lord is on our side
No wonder we were certain and so sure
Of quenching our thirst with water so pure.

The devil and apostles used to encircle us
They used to enwreathe us about
But in the name of the Lord
Almighty Father, we have banjaxed,
Stonkered, and scuttled them all.

For a time, darkness looked on
Suddenly, "Cock-a-doodle-doo," a rooster crowed
Darkness disappeared
And I knew it was my morning
Directing all kinds of fish to my net.

Look beyond a bad past
Strive for a better tomorrow.

Avoid jealousy
A source of hate.

Let peace be a badge
Wear it at home
In the city,
In the field,
And when you travel.

Thou hast become your own enemy,
Thou hast doubted the potential
Of a tree planted by the riverside.

Now sanguine about my own harvest
I comprehend the sum of what my eyes saw not
About gifts,
I comprehend the total of what many ears hear not
On gifts
Just give another and another will bless you.

144

It is not about how fast the food is cooked,
But how well it is cooked

Great players create opportunities,
Wise people take worthy chances.

Speak less when you are angry,
For an angry person is not a reliable person.

A tree with sense gives fruit to another
And receives abundant rain and sun from another.

A cent or dollar gift to a reliable charity,
A gift so genuine in a worldly stage where
Abundance chases wise actors who
Outperform actors who have not comprehended yet.

I wrote my blessings down this morning
And I was amazed at all the things that God did for
me.

I tried a new thing
I got a new result.

If your friends' actions
Are repugnant to moral justice
Be careful.

If your friends actions
Are insensitive to others pain
Leave them alone.

147

You thought you were in bad
Shape until you met people
In worse shape.

You are not a failure simply because
you got back up.

If your friends actions
Disobey authority
Avoid them.

If you want to change your group,
Start by changing yourself.

The courage you need most
Is the courage to start.

If their actions
Encourage education
Hold 'em tight.

Why should someone else believe
In you when you doubt yourself constantly.

If his or her action thinks
Bad drugs are cool
Call him or her a fool.

The energy expended worrying about
What you have not
Could be spent rejoicing for what
You have.

If their actions
Discourage love for others
Be careful with them.

Success can only be defined
By you.

I want to improve on my character
Before improving on my reputation because God is
interested in my character but my ego is interested
in my reputation.

If God and family
Are meaningless to your associates,
Reevaluate your association.

If their actions seem hopeless
Run away, runaway baby.

It is just nice to be nice.

Life is like a game
You are the referee of your life
Your life is controlled by each
Whistle you blow.

If thinking by itself makes
A winner, then everybody is
A winner because we all think.

Think positively and execute
Your positive thoughts.

God, a source for any resource, I believe
Supplies all your needs, if you believe.

If your problems go home with you
All the time, your home will have problems
All the time.

To a society, you may be just a man
But to your group or your family
You are a king for the things
You supply and things you manage.

In all educational build-up and
In all academic pile-up
Harmonize it with a degree in
wisdom/understanding
From the University of Heaven
In manifestation of a super force for
All realms.

Love progresses but enmity retrogresses.

What worked for Mr. And Mrs. A and made
Them happy may not work for Mr. And Mrs. Z.

Learning from your mistakes
The devil has paid double
For the pain and all the trouble.

A pretty morning has come, fully loaded
With a unique and special kind of upgrade.

In pursuit of a God endorsed goal, they will
criticize,
But let not their criticism occupy a space in your
mind
For that same group that called you strange will call
you amazing if your effort pays off.

156

The birds are singing about my morning,
The Davids are already dancing about my morning,
My morning is plain and self-explanatory,
A morning with love, joy, and full of glory.

You can drink
From the fountain of uniqueness
You can swim
In the ocean of happiness.

If they did not love you when you were bad
And still don't love you now that you have changed,
They probably have a problem with your creator.

If praising God makes the devil mad
But gives you control,
Make him mad and take control.

If raising your hands to the almighty
Offends Satan,
Offend Satan.

If going to church bothers some folks
Bother those folks.

It is honorable to have credit
But it is dishonorable to live on credit.

Food always on the table
A sign of God who is able.

If valuing positive diversity provokes
Be proud it provokes.

If losing weight enhances your self-esteem
Enhance your self-esteem.

The overestimation of the iniquitous energy
Is the underestimation of the positive energy.

If showing love makes you feel supreme
Feel supreme.

In God's training camp
Less came as a training technique,
Abundance followed as a tool,
Sharpened by Heaven to overrule.

A roof over our head
Confirmation of what God said.

In thy going out,
You wear a princely emblem
In thy coming in,
You declare the glory of God.

161

Uneasy plans schemed to curtail you
Weakened.

The only way to start becoming what you aspire
Is to start becoming.

Ammunition maximized to derail you
Zeroed out.

Efforts strategized to keep you down
Head for disintegration.

Seeds of faith in germinating stages
Draw unfriendly attention.

Your river gradually turning to blue ocean with
varieties therein
Awakes the devil's fear.

The only solution to attacking a problem
Is to start attacking the problem.

Faith now activated
Marches you forward and forward
Toward a reward
For those seeds gallantly sown
In a fertile soil.

During the day, thou coruscates,
Under the sun, you flash
At nighttime, thou glares
Under moonlight, you glitter.

Nothing will occur
Until you make it occur.

Winners use adversity
To their own advantage.

The way, your businesses treat their clients,
And cater to their needs
Determine your share of the community's economic
harvests.

In spite of a sick body and large crowd,
She tried
To touch the hem of Jesus' garment.

Despite size and incredible weapon,
He tried
To annihilate Goliath with a slingshot.

Even though Zacheus was invisible in a crowd,
He tried
To lay eyes on Jesus, by climbing a tree.

You may not enter an Ivy League college
But you're in a college.

You may not pray like the reverend prays
But you communicate with God.

You may not be able to write like Shakespeare
But you expressed your thoughts.

You may not be able to sing like him or her
But you sing

You may not be able to teach like Jesus
But you share ideas.

Time for planning
Is different from time for execution.

People are attracted to ideologies
That solve their problems.

In a fish dominated ocean,
A woebegone fished only wood.

In a world of uncertainty
A defeatist prays not.

169

In a world of give and take
A forsaken only takes.

In a time of peace
A reckless fusses.

In a world where you don't know
Until you try
A downhearted tries not.

In a place where education is free
A disconsolate gets none.

In God's presence, your color matters less
Even thou he made color and no rectifying.

In God's kingdom, your intelligence is baseless
Because he authors wisdom and understanding.

Like a wise antelope, I spotted the lion and ran
I ran, ran, ran, towards a bright light
And the light rescued me
And made me wiser

In a time of upliftment
A dolt discourages.

In a world filled with beautiful creations and colors
A pessimist says there's no God.

Each time the devil said that I couldn't do it,
God said I could.

Spend more time on solutions
Than on problems.

A better today I can describe vividly,
And try forgetting yesterday
Which is unworthy of my sadness.

Created children of the world are dying,
Identified children degrade immeasurably,
And we search for unidentified flying objects.

Those who doubt your ability directly
Doubt the ability of your God directly.

There is a reward for everything done well.

The person who is still hesitant to give
Has not read Luke 6:38, Proverbs19: 17 and Acts
20:35.

There is no value to your dream
Until you act on it.

As the anticipated time draws near,
The iniquitous energy looks silly,
Controlling and feasting on fear,
A wise person plants in the summer, fall, even when
chilly
A good person blossoms incredibly without tear.

175

Let not your knockdown
Be a knockout.

The value of faith appreciates
Each time you act upon it.

My obligations and portions have I kept,
Love and respect have I given,
Confident that a prayer has swept
All competition in a match so power driven
That an ego bled and all pride wept.

A Christian that treats the poor with cruelty has not
read Proverbs 17:5 or Proverbs 21:13.

Channel your frustration
To positive action.

Super leaders consider everybody's suggestion
Until the suggestions are no longer needed.

But I know come tomorrow,
With our plan directed by heaven,
We'll laugh; we'll praise,
And we'll sip on ice water.

Your faith and hope paid off,
Your good desire quenches not,
Your dreams suffer not, your loaded ship just
blasted off.

If you are mean to the poor,
Proverbs 14:21 questions your Christianity.

In that pleasing world that I hanker for,
A rich shares wealth as commoners ditch,
Poverty is a bottomless pit without ground,
As hope and happiness in all faces found.

In a world that I desire
Good speech works to alleviate pain and outreach
To all needs, that is enough crowned.
Satisfaction for all is then year round.

You trash Proverb 21:13
When you mistreat the poor.

179

How can the door open
When you have not knocked?

In a beautiful world I yearn for
Each constantly explores a way to reach another's
need
So selfishness is bound.
Sharing becomes a duty as harvest abound.

Why tell everybody what you are planning to do
When everybody will eventually find out
When you are done.

The greatest quote of all is: "God loves you"

What you call snack, may be somebody's dinner
elsewhere.
Something to think about.

To heaven have I looked up for aid,
A sigh of relief each time heaven said,
" It is alright."

Sometimes it takes longer than I expected,
But in all, goodness and mercy I collected.

The good of the talks are all I hear,
For the bad of the talks instigate a fear.

You may get more if you are appreciative and
thankful
For the one you already received.

If you are able to do it one time
You'll be able to do it all the time.

You may not be able to cook the delicacies like her
But you can at least boil water for her.

It takes one additional penny to make 99 cents a
dollar,
Every penny is important.

Selective listening makes peace the way
For love and self-aggrandizement to stay.

God's way
Is the only way out of this mess.

There is something to gain
When you learn to work with people *positively*
different from you.

When the blind worked together with the deaf
As a team,
All written information to them was read perfectly
And all the voice information was heard perfectly.

Combine your strengths
And you will make a difference.

Encircle by the Holy Ghost,
A sudden attack,
Deterred,
A planned attack,
Marred,
A victory celebration planned.

Fresh energy and assurance are stirred,
To soar me to the greatest altitude.

Kindness well learned and inherited,
If misinterpreted as weakness,
So be it and let it be.

Where God's umbrella folds not,
Is where I want to sit.

It is very biblical to be
Sensitive to others pain and need.

Where everyone can do all things through Christ
Is what we have to build.

Be not upset when a person asks you to repeat what
you said,
Because that person may have admired the way you
just said it.

187

Where size, looks, age, color, origin matters not
Is where love lives.

Laugh not at anyone who cannot effectively do what
you do
Because you may not effectively do what he/she
does.

Anytime you
Or your business
Is adaptive to others culture,
You are bound to gain
Cooperation from such culture.

Where grace abounds
Is where I want to be.

Where God's mercy endureth
Is where I take shelter.

It is progressive to separate someone's offense
From his/her cultural background.

189

Always strive to be a good example
No matter what position you hold in a group setting.

Where God's riches supply needs
Is where I stand.

A great leader acknowledges that
A person's difference can actually mean his or her
strength to the team.

Where peacemakers are called God's children
Is where I belong.

Where envy is not sin
Is where I forbid.

Everybody is responsible for what goes on in a
business or group setting.

God's law on mistreatment should
Override national laws on mistreatment.

God's law that you don't know
May be hurting you.

Where the merciful obtains mercy
Is where I cherish.

A wise manager or supervisor
Considers his/her workers as team members
And not as unfortunate subordinates.

Some managers or heads consider themselves as
team leaders
And not as superiors.

Bear in mind that behavioral standards are not
universal
What is accepted in South America may not be
accepted in South Africa.

Why laugh at the way someone tries to speak your
language
When you cannot even say that person's name right.

Even Pele and Michael Jordan
Took advice from their coaches.

World covenant has not been kept
Peace forgotten and utterly forsaken
We ponder, we wonder, we wept
For gross selfishness, and bitterness, is awaken.

If you obey Jesus' commands
He considers you a friend.

It's fulfilling to observe the inspiring rectitude
Of these angels sent to my house.

The only way that you can teach a subject
Is to learn the subject first.

Harvest abounds
In every appreciative barn.

Only wise people
Accumulate in drought.

Teachers are still teaching,
Preachers are still preaching,
Mentors are still mentoring,
Water abound in quantity and in quality,
Yet the fool is thirsty.

May not know exactly what path God leads us next
Precisely, all I see is abundance.

May not comprehend a favor's release or retention
Accurately, all I feel is goodness.

I am the best individual
To explain my relationship with God.

Gratefulness,
An emblem,
Worthy to be worn,
Rain or shine.

All successful people have the same thing in
common:
Perseverance, hard work, belief in God, belief in
self, and love for what they do.

As a devil watches helplessly,
Battles led by General God
Are successful in entirety.
Walls are falling,
My Goliaths are fallen,
To rise no more.

To a tobacco company
Has his seeds gone to,
Deteriorating a lung so needed,
Being unfair with a gift.

Focusing on no good but negatives,
Desisting from calling myself blessed
To please you and your ego,
Is disrelishing to heavenly justice.

Wait for no man
To boast your spirit.

That bad habit that you refused to get rid of
Will eventually get rid of you.

A shoe too big or too small for your feet affects
your walk.

If that relationship is not meant for you,
Stay away or it will affect your walk.

By your standard and measurement
I may not have enough yet,
But I sure know what and whom I have
And I'm persuaded that he is able to move me
above, across, and beyond.

Habits that waited to devour have vanished,
to darkness they're faded,
and into brightness deliverance packages
await patiently.

An alcohol drinking has been pressured by heaven
It has taken to its heel
It has gone into the dark.

Now wipe tears, weep no more,
A plagued land is about to laugh,
Unstoppable rain has been ordered,
For Jah has degreed a good news.

Evaluate me not by yesterday's mistake,
But by today and tomorrow's greatness.

Giving in to the enemy is dangerous
But genuine defense is no bad indication.

If it appears no door is opening
Wait and have patience
With prayers in charge
A double door will open
As choice fights for a chance
Select you the best
From two so blessed
Celebrate a conquest
With a praise so impressed.

I desire to enter all promised lands
I pray
To go and be of great service
To all You delegate me day by day.

I plan to unplan if it is not God's perfect will.

Encompass and mold me like Jesus
Whose style and walk made a way,
For the ordinary creature to have a voice
In a kingdom that presents a pay and a choice
Equally to all princes and princesses.

Exchange thou not peace, love for detrimental
tension
And rough times that embrace days and nights or
wartime craze
And let peace and love be the theme for your
convention.

An association that lacks morality
Lacks substance

An ultimate guide,
An ultimate directive,
An ultimate regulation,
An ultimate advisor,
An ultimate instructor,
A handbook,
A bible.

Worry thee less about criticism
And give decreased attention to war
But if pushed too far,
Drop all ammunition, pray and praise
Intensively like Paul and Silas
To attract a heavenly intervention.

N4 = RP (Necessary 4 = Rounded Personality)
God + Family + Church + School = Rounded
Personality.

Care ye less about temporarily looking stupid at
their speculation
For beloved Mary, Jesus' mother looked stupid
those days as a pregnant virgin.
Thank God for divine conception.

I am always happy to be happy.

It is not biblical to love others more than your
spouse/ children or family.

It is biblical to love others as you love yourself.

Let peace and love manifest your sophistication this
season,
And let all ill concern fade and phase away into the
dark
And leave wars to the Master of apprehension.

May be hard to forget
But we must forgive and forget
Forgiveness, a key to heaven's door
Forgetting, a balm for war sore.

Even though Sushi is good
I have not craved for Sushi,
Because I have not tried Sushi.

Love you positively,
Abhor you negativity
Show love, and be a blessing
And let's enjoy in harmony.

How better your works had become,
Your light will not fame out,
It has drawn might and strength.

208

Your pieced heart
Now fully healed
Has sealed your crushed bone together.

How better your life had become for a rematch and
victory,
Your faith will not fade out
It has pulled a conqueror,
A lion of Judah.

Father, they doeth evil, we know
But only if thou alloweth them.

Selfishness and anger abound here on earth
Father, who is Omnipresent, stand by me.

Human beings are wingless
Because they are not meant to fly.

Thou standeth by me day and night
I will not fear.

The things God has done are marvelous in our eyes.
Let the universe therefore look at us and affirm that,
Forever Omnipresent Stands By You (FOSBY).

Attack a status quo with patience, persistence and
progressive ideas.

She's of course a rounded CCL
Constantly scaring the devil to hell
A Classy Christian Lady
Will still be classy even at 80.

That individual that you hate and call derogatory names today may be the best individual to assist you tomorrow.

—

She is so satisfied,
Need always supplied,
By God always magnified,
At all times, she praises,
For all things she prays.

There is no sense waiting to excel in that,
Which is ungodly.

Good management is not only about getting good
workers.
It is also about getting good workers to stay, work
together and produce quality output.

It is rewarding to be
Full of joy when in need
Full of glow when in plenty
Full of thanks in time of peace
Full of love in time of war.

People who are generally loved or liked by other
people,
Have love already occupying a space in their heart.

213

She glows,
She knows,
Always sowing a good seed,
With abundant reaping guaranteed.

In inexpensive outfit,
She appears too legit,
In expensive attire
Can't help but admire.

You are not really ahead in a game or a race
Until the final whistle is blown.

Even when quiet,
She epitomizes angelic sight
Confident and careful
Graceful and joyful.

You can help someone become smart
If you keep calling him or her smart.

Listen to all talks that your parents, your pastors,
your teachers, your counselors, your supervisors,
and your prophets have to say. May sound illogical
To you today, but will become logical Tomorrow.

215

She is classy and Godly
A combination so highly
Treasured for her heavenly traits of sensibility,
ability, and versatility.

Even when quiet
You epitomize an angelic sight
Confident and careful
Graceful and joyful.

Ask first for wisdom to handle "enough"
So that "enough and excess" will not blow your
mind.

A child that obeys his or her parents
Will be obeyed by his or her children when he or
she becomes a parent.

A Christian mama is
Firm but not mean,
Calm but not intimidated,
Tough but not rough,
Fanatical and so Pentecostal.

What degree of help and respect that you accord
your parents, supervisor, pastor, or manager is the
degree you'll be accorded when your time arrives.

217

Be not upset with one that sprays saliva when
speaking
Because he maybe having a malady.

A blatherskite without God
Is like a toothless bulldog.

A braggart or boastful talker without God
Is a loquacious fool.

218

Faith, forgiveness, discipline, and loving kindness is
after all what Christianity is all about.

Angels are sent to my house
Some are pretty and sagacious
Some are handsome and chivalrous
Each is fortified and prepared
All are equipped and fully loaded.

Baby
Starring at you constantly
No artificiality I see.

Please smile at my direction
Only if it is from your heart,
For a fake smile arouses my curiosity.

Dignity and class override a fuss.

A silent response is so dignified
In a place peace is so glorified.

With a prayer in control,
Humiliate those deficiencies
That seem to bind.

To utterly believe
What you've not seen, is like
Placing a value, or a claim on what is to come.

Thank you lord, for opening my eyes wider to see
love, not hate.

Take that crooked dollar
And give me a straight dime.

God, I thank you for broadening my mind deeper,
Deeper to appreciate you more,
Deeper to put your first.

Lord, I cannot offer you a drink,
for thou drinketh not,
I cannot offer you food, for thou eateth not,
So I am saying, "Thank you, sir."

One array of the rainbow is vibrant,
Together
All arrays are exciting, stimulating
And imposing.

Don't be nice to people only when you want
something from them.

I cried, like Solomon,
I cried for magnificent lead and guide,
With humility and no pride,
I receive the abundant wisdom supplied.

I rather be a small shot in a friendly environment
Than be a big shot in a hostile setting.

I stand, claim, and believe on today's wisdom and
Receive,
Forthcoming wisdom expressed to
Relieve,
The pain of some that still
Grieve.

Love,
It does not constrain light,
It does not restrain growth, it takes away envy,
It takes away bitterness.

Those businesses or ministries that you call "large
and successful" used to be "small and doubtful."

It takes time
It takes faith
It takes perseverance to succeed.

Love,
It fertilizes your soil,
It organizes your seed,
It fuels your light constantly,
It nourishes your soul incessantly.

A team leader must be ready to deliver all he promised his team for achieving a particular goal.

It pays to be happy.

The ability to persist and not give up is the secret to reaching our destination.

Love,
It makes a way,
It brightens your future.

Love of God;
It give you joy
It gives you peace.

Our importance is not based on what we
accumulated, it is based on how many lives we
impacted.

227

Success, in the highest order,
Shows up when you think hope is gone.

The formula for success is "keep on trying".

If you expect premium,
You have to give premium.

Good things that last never come easy.
Hard work, and persistence, is the only way.

You don't necessarily have to be well known to
make it in life:
Whatever it is you are doing,
Just do it well.

You are not successful if you are not happy.

Can we walk in unity and obedience
As in the time of Jericho
When unity and obedience broke barriers?

To your difference, I'll look beyond
To your positive uniqueness, will I embrace.

From whence cometh E. Coli's enemy?
Not from Jupiter, but clean hands, cloths, utter
sanitation, and thorough cooking.

Listeria Monocytogen,
Your hatred for adequately heated food is no lie
As your dislike for sanitary conditions is no
fallacy.

I tried not to imagine
I only endeavor to reason
At the devil's lost chance
In heaven over ignorance.

I dig no more
For answers to my papa's progressive actions
I now know for sure
That enmity retrogresses, but love progresses.

The devil's fire burns incessantly
Yet no heat we feel.

The devil has slashed with a sword,
Still no blood we see.

As we worship and celebrate Jesus
May we represent what He represents.

May we love all that Jesus loves;
Love, peace, and giving.

Creation, I know it is
Evolution, some think it is.

Am I not supposed to thank Thee plentifully before
grumbling for moon and star that I want.

233

Catechize no more on my negatives
Explore at large on my positives.

If you loathe the way she looks
Sorry, I can't help you
Because the sagacious lady is not yours
Of course, the chivalrous lady is virtuous.

It is disgusting
When you stack, and pile your visions
With no actions.

I cannot play instruments like DavidSolomonKings
But I can make sounds of praise.

It is repugnant
When dreams are destroyed
By fear of mortal disapproval.

In the absence of worldly connections
My praise and worship linked me to greater
connections.

You do not have to down grade someone
In order to up grade yourself.

Where God's anointing shatters yoke
Is where I see.

It is not beauteous
When faith stands alone
Without works.

It is even an abomination
When good people diminish for lack of courage
For that person who avoids making mistakes also
avoids growing up in life
Spiritually, materially, and physically
For that man or woman who has not grown lately
Has not tried something new lately.

I believe in the inside beauty, but the first thing your
intending husband sees is physical beauty.
So fix yourself to the best of your ability.

It is unbiblical to say, " I love you" without showing
love through
Prayer, support, and sharing.

What you have made up your mind to become
Is what you will actually become.

Just try

Success without the wisdom of God is like a water
tank with an invisible leak.
When you wake up in the morning, the water in
your tank is gone and you cannot tell why.

The road to Success Avenue is narrow
But Success Avenue is wide.

Utterly blessed,
We adamantly refused to be stressed.

I will be grateful if you give me a dime today.
I will be more grateful if you show me how to make
a dollar tomorrow.

A son that comes close to his wise father
Ends up being wise.

A daughter that helps mama in the kitchen all the
time,
Ends up being a good cook.

A person that has a good relationship with God
Acquireth favor.

If we make our parents happy
They will make us happy.

If we make God happy by being obedient,
Then He will make us happy.

Encompass yourself with the individuals who want
you to be successful.

241

Avoid all avoidables because
Some people are worse than Judas;
They'll betray you without asking for money.

The bible is the indispensable manual for
motivation.

Motivate yourself adequately and have meaningful
success.

What goes into a child's head today
Help mold him/her for tomorrow.

Buy what you can afford
And not what you cannot afford.

Obedience draws rewards.

Today's hand wash is tomorrow's savings on medical bills.

Exclude the unwanted & include the needed

Sharing transcends all aspects of love.

Happy employees produce happy results.

If you keep trying, you'll become.

Unhappy input produces unhappy output.

To be the best father or husband,
Is a leadership role in the highest

To be the best mother or wife
Is a management role of immense dignity

You cannot let the one percent insufficiency
Outshine the 99 percent sufficiency

Acknowledgements

When God is ready to use you for a purpose, He sends people your way. I thank God for these people and organizations.

The entire Ufomadu family; Pastor Efell & Sister Brenda Williams and Tabernacle of Praise Church; Check-2-Cash, Inc.; the Staff of Prudence Mortgage Funding LLC; Paula White Ministries; Dr. Emmanuel & Patience Oranika; Dixie Loan & Mortgage Inc.; Chief Accountant of Wares Ferry Accounting Firm, Daniel Anyanwu, CPA; Roger & Denise Dukes of Ministering Monologues; Regions Bank Branch Manager, Liz Rutledge, and other employees; Kingsley Iyobebe, Director of K & S Financial Group; Investment Executive of Prime Vest Financial Services, Julie M. Simmons, CFP; Mr. & Mrs. Uche Okereke; Vaughn Regional Medical Center employees; Kakson Ltd.; Pastor Vickers and Christian Life Church; J T Networks; Fosby International;

DECE Transport; my friends working for the Department of Agriculture & Industries for the State of Alabama; Rev. & Mrs. Carl Thurman; Councilwoman Bennie Crenshaw; Selma Times Journal; God's Time International; Faith Christian Gallery in Selma; Assemblies of God; Dr. & Mrs. Osasere Aghedo and ENT Consultants in Selma;

R.L. Zeigler, Inc. Management and employees; the entire Arondizuogu family, Deeper Life Church; Dr. Ernest Okeke; Barbara Sanders; Dr. Michael Durry; Dr. Patricia Kendrick Robinson and Pediatric & Adolescent Medicine, Inc.; the director of Docce Group; Dr. & Mrs. Lekan Ayanwele; Ralph Gibbs; Nwoji family, the entire Umuahia family; Mr. and Mrs. Mike Modozie; Dr. Timothy Marlow; James and Glenda Williams; Dr. & Mrs. David Okeowo; Dr. & Mrs. Zeph Okonkwo; Dr. & Mrs. Paul Erhunmwunsee; Dr. & Mrs. Benjamin C. Datiri ; Dr. & Mrs. David Iyegha; Mr. & Mrs. Paul Oyegbeda; Dr. K. Olibe; Dr. & Mrs. Chuddy Okeye; Mr & Mrs. Chris Ataghuman; Mr. & Mrs.

*Ndem Onwuka; Mr. & Mrs. Godwin
Oji; Mr. & Mrs. Lawrence Kromtit;
Dr. & Mrs. Julius Brown; Laura Brown;
Mrs. C. Pickett; Emmanuel Iwuoha;
Robert & Janice Martin; Mrs. D.
Holifield; Oge Onuoha; Mr. & Mrs.
Sam Ehie; the Egbuna family; Principal
of Edgewood Elementary, Concetta
Burton; Principal of Selma Middle
C.H.A.T. Academy, Charlotte Griffeth;
Principal of Selma High School, Joe J.
Peterson, Jr.; Manager of Arnold's
Bakery, Vera Anyanwu; U. Nzeakor
group; Small Business Development
Center; Ohuhu group; Utimo Org./hotels;
Felix Ijeoma group; The Ezumah family;
The Umuohuonu family; Ricky and Vicky
Brown, owner of Anointed Styles; Davis*

Family Medicine, P.C.; Chief Consultant of Emmanuel & E. Accounting Corporation, Emmanuel Epeagba.

About the Author

Dr. Udo F. Ufomadu, Ph.D., is the Managing Director of Ufomadu Consulting Services (UCS), a business consulting firm based in Selma, Alabama. The firm specializes in business planning, expense curtailment, asset& team building. He is the author of the highly acclaimed <u>Anthology of Inspiration.</u>

Dr. Ufomadu has 13 years of experience as a Consumer Food Safety Protection Specialist working with business management in regulatory and inspection capacity for the state of Alabama. He reviews and verifies food industry procedures in HACCP/SSOP plans relative to consumer protection and safety.

He is trained and certified in handling diversity in the work place. He

255

obtained a Ph.D. in Business Administration from Madison University, a Master of Science in Administration and Supervision from Alabama State University, additional Master courses in Personnel Management from Troy State, and a Bachelor of Science in Business Administration/Management from Troy State University.

Dr. Udo Ufomadu was inducted as a member of the Institute of Management Consultants (IMC) in 2002. He is a professional member of American Management Association (AMA) and a professional member of the Institute of Food Technologists (IFT). He is also a member of Tabernacle of Praise Church in Selma.

Dr. Ufomadu, also an award-winning inspirational poet, consults nationally and internationally.

If you need help or more information you may
contact Ufomadu Consulting Services at:

Ufomadu Consulting & Publishing (U C & P)
P. O. Box 746
Selma, AL. 36702-0746

Telephone: 334-418-0088

An excerpt from author's previous book,
<u>Anthology of Inspiration: Poem the Best Out of You</u>.

<u>Success Avenue</u>

The window of my soul
Has opened to curiosity
Where is Success Avenue?
Sometimes we ponder
Many before us pondered too
Road to Success Avenue is narrow
Yet Success Avenue is wide
On many occasions
Some have ventured to widen the road
But fell short
Some have refused to see their success
Even when evident
Many have refused to become successful
Even when capable
So challenging have these past
Years become
When men drenched in good desire
Seek to be successful in
natural and spiritual
When decent men explore in search
For perfection
When good women
ransack their path
When decent children ferret
A world for Success Avenue